THE

INSTANT POT

RECIPES

COOKBOOK

Fresh & Foolproof Electric Pressure Cooker Recipes Made for The Everyday Home & Your Instant Pot.

(Electric Pressure Cooker Cookbook) (Instant Pot Cookbook)

BY

SHELLEY FOREMAN

Table of Contents

INTRODUCTION

My passion for pressure cooking runs deep. If you have cooked with a pressure cooker, then you will be familiar with this kitchen appliance. It is a multi-cooker that performs more than seven functions. The Instant Pot enables you to cook a wide variety of dishes including meat, fish, eggs, grain, poultry, beans, cakes, yogurt and vegetables etc. What makes the Instant Pot exceptional is because you can use different cooking programs such as a steamer, rice cooker, sauté pan, and even a warming pot, thus saving more time, money, and space than buying any other kitchen appliances.

The Instant Pot serves as a multi-use programmable appliance that can help create easy, fast and delicious recipes with the ability to apply different cooking settings all in one pot. It was developed by clever Canadian technology experts seeking to be the ultimate kitchen devices, from stir-frying, pressure cooking, slow cooking and yogurt and cake making. It was created to serve as a one-stop shop to allow home cooks prepare a flavorful meal with the press of a button. You can cook almost everything in your Instant Pot.

In this book, we will explore the variety of easy delicious dishes you can cook with your Instant Pot. We will explore a wide variety of dishes, from breakfast to dinner, soups to stews, desserts to appetizers, meat to beef, side dishes to vegetables and use a healthy ingredient in the process. The vast majority of the recipes can be prepared and served in less than 45 minutes. Each recipe is written with the exact preparation time, cooking instructions and ingredients required to prepare the dishes. Once you try these delicious dishes with our cookbook, you and your Instant Pot are sure to become inseparable too.

Meaning Of an Instant Pot

The Instant Pot is a multifunctional cooker that acts as a slow cooker, rice cooker, steamer, electric pressure cooker, sauté pan and a yogurt maker. It is a single kitchen appliance or multi-cooker that does the job of seven different kitchen appliances ranging from electric pressure cooker, rice cooker, steamer, yogurt maker, sauté pan, and warming pot etc. It functions with the combination of steam and pressure which enables your foods to cook quicker and safer than other kitchen devices. It is a programmable countertop multi-cooker which speeds up cooking by 2~6 times using up to 70% less energy.

The Instant Pot can cook nutritious healthy food in a convenient and consistent fashion, making everything from slow-and-low barbecue dishes, stews, rice pilaf, lentil, bacon, chicken and steamed veggies. The Instant Pot deserves a spot in your kitchen because you can rely on it more than any other kitchen devices.

The Instant Pot is a versatile multi-cooker that can execute the function of a pressure cooker, slow cooker, rice cooker, steamer, poultry and more. It has lots of safety features which makes it safer to use and comes in different models. It comes with preset programs that are specifically designed to cook your food to perfection, whether it be a chicken, desserts, cheesecake, a stew, soup, or porridge.

1. Saving Time & Energy:

The Instant Pot cook foods much faster than any other traditional methods of cooking. Electric pressure cooker can reduce cooking time by up to 70% when compared with any other traditional methods of cooking. Cooking with an Instant Pot requires less water used in cooking and much less energy is required thereby saving up to 70% of energy comparing with boiling, steaming, and slow cooking.

You will save more time and money when cooking with an Instant Pot. An Instant Pot can cook a whole chicken in just half an hour, cook a tender pot roast in less than 2 hours, make a large squash in just 10 minutes and veggies in less than 5 thereby saving more time, energy and money.

2 Preserving Nutrients & Cook Tasty Food:

Pressure cooking ensures that heat is evenly and quickly distributed while cooking. The food is not necessarily required to be immersed in water, it simply requires sufficient water to keep the electric pressure cooker filled with steam. The vitamins and minerals will not be dissolved or leached away by water. Because the food is surrounded with the steam, the foods will not be oxidized by air exposure at heat, so asparagus, lentil, broccoli, artichoke, and other veggies retain their bright green colors and phytochemicals. It will also enable the food to retain its original flavor.

Scientific studies have proved that pressure cooking is the best method for retaining the vitamins and minerals of the food that your body needs. Pressure cooking broccoli, for instance, will retain 90% of its vitamin C. The retention when compared to boiling is (66% retention) or steaming (78%). Instant Pot tends to be the healthier option.

3 Eliminating Harmful Micro-Organisms in Food:

Foods are pressure cooked at a temperature above the boiling point of water, killing almost all harmful living micro-organisms such as bacteria, fungi, and viruses. It helps to destroy all harmful micro-organisms that are toxic to your health. Some foods such as rice, wheat, corn and beans may carry fungal poisons called aflatoxins.

Aflatoxins are naturally occurring mycotoxins produced by some species of Aspergillus fungi, as a result of improper storage, such as in humid conditions. Research has proved that aflatoxins are a potent trigger of liver cancer and may play a vital role in a host of other cancers too. Aflatoxins cannot be destroyed by just heating your food to the boiling point, they can only be destroyed by pressure cooking.

4 Helps Boost Digestibility of Foods:

I believe you must have heard, "You are what you eat." But actually, you are what you absorb from your food. Boosting the digestibility of your food will maximize the nutritional value to your body. Pressure cooking your food makes the toughest meats moist and tender, which is the key to foods that your body can easily digest and absorb.

1 **Soup:**

The Instant Pot has a soup program that is 30 minutes on High Pressure. The Soup feature depends on if you are using fresh or frozen meats. The soup times may range from 20 minutes to an hour. The setting cooks at High Pressure for about 30 minutes. It can be adjusted to more to cook for about 40 minutes. It can also be adjusted to less to cook for about 20 minutes.

2 **Meat / Stew:**

The meat / stew program is 20 minutes on High Pressure. Though, the cooking times may vary depending on the temperature, size, and thickness of the meats. The Meat / Stew function cooks at High Pressure for about 35 minutes. It can be adjusted to more cooks for about 45 minutes and Adjusted to less cooks for about 20 minutes.

3 **Bean / Chili:**

The Bean / Chili program is 30 minutes on High Pressure. The Bean / Chili feature cooks at High Pressure for 30 minutes. It can be adjusted to more cooks for about 40 minutes. The button can also be adjusted to less cooks for about 25 minutes.

4 **Poultry:**

The poultry button is 12 minutes on High Pressure. This cooking time is meant for small portions of uncooked chicken. Larger portions of chicken will require a cooking time of about 25 minutes to reach a center temperature of 165°F. The Poultry function cooks at High Pressure for 15 minutes. The button can be adjusted to more cooks for about 30 minutes and Adjusted to less cooks for about 5 minutes.

5 **Slow Cook:**

The Slow Cook button can be programmed from between 30 minutes to 20 hours and the cooking time can be lowered up to 24 hours. The Slow Cook mode can be set to normal (which is equivalent to low), more (which is equivalent to high), or less (which is equivalent to keep warm mode).

6 **Sauté:**

The sauté button can be used to brown your meat inside your Instant Pot. The temperature of the sauté feature can be adjusted by using the 'Adjust' function to cycle through the modes of less, normal, and more. The temperature mode needs to be adjusted within 10 seconds of pressing the sauté feature. When you press the Sauté function, kindly wait until it displays "Hot" before adding your ingredients into the pot.

7 **Pressure:**

The pressure setting works as a toggle between Low and High-Pressure function. It can simply be used to switch between High and Low-pressure settings for different pressure cooking programs.

8 Manual:

The Manual feature can be used to start pressure cooking. It can be used to switch between low and high pressure by using the 'pressure' function within 10 seconds of pressing the 'Manual' button. You can set a pressure level and cook time using the Adjust and [+] or [-] buttons. When the time is up, the timer will begin to count down.

9 Adjust:

This button can be used to adjust the temperature of the slow cooking and sauté settings between less, normal, and more. This button can be used to toggle from the Less, Normal and More settings. You can select any of the feature you wish to use and press Adjust until the light under Less, Normal and More is adjusted to the desired setting.

10 Timer:

The timer setting is for programmed delayed cooking. The button performs the function for both slow cooking mode and regular pressure cooking mode. This setting must be pressed within 10 seconds of setting your cooking program's time and can be adjusted by pressing the + and − buttons.

11 Keep Warm / Cancel:

The Keep Warm button can be used to set the unit into keep warm mode, and another less turns the unit OFF. This setting helps to turn the Auto Keep Warm function ON and OFF. The Keep Warm function keeps the foods in your cooking pot between 145–172°F. This button can also be used to cancel a function or to turn off the Instant Pot.

12 Yogurt:

This function is not included in the IP-LUX series and is a fully-automated program. This feature can be used to make yogurt. You can press this button and Adjust to More for boiling the milk and use Normal for incubating the yogurt.

13 Steam:

This button cooks at High Pressure for about 10 minutes. It can be Adjusted to more cooks for about 15 minutes and Adjusted to less for about 3 minutes. The Steam function is simply normal High-Pressure mode that can be lowered down to 0 minutes. You can perform a quick release once the cooking time is up. This function is very important when cooking leafy vegetables and prevents them from being overcooked.

14 Porridge:

The Porridge button cooks at High Pressure for 20 minutes. It can be adjusted to more cooks for 30 minutes and Adjusted to less cooks for 15 minutes.

15 Multigrain:

The Multigrain button cooks at High Pressure for about 40 minutes. It can be adjusted to more cooks for 45 minutes and pressure cooking time of about 60 minutes. It can also be adjusted to less cooks for about 20 minutes.

16 Rice:

The Rice button is an automated function that begins at 12 minutes. This button functions at low pressure and can cook white or jasmine rice in about 20 minutes flat. The setting is specifically designed for cooking white rice and the cooking time can be adjusted depending on the quantity of water and rice in the cooking pot.

17 Egg:

The Egg button cooks at High Pressure for about 5 minutes. The button can be adjusted to more cooks for about 6 minutes and Adjusted to less cooks for about 4 minutes.

18 Cake:

The Cake button cooks at High Pressure for about 30 minutes. It can be adjusted to more cooks for about 40 minutes and Adjusted to less cooks for about 25 minutes.

The Instant Pot comes along with lots of accessories. You might need to buy more accessories to get the most out of your meals:

1. **Silicone Egg Mold:**

The silicon egg mold will fit in your 5, 6, 8-quart pressure cookers. It can be used for storing smaller portions of dishes and includes a sealing lid.

2. **Silicone Mini Mitts:**

It is advisable to protect your fingers with the mini mitts. The cooking pot usually gets hot when cooking, the mini mitts set can be used to protect your hands when lifting items out of your pressure cooker.

3. **Silicone Vegetable Steamer and Lifter:**

The steamer / lifter keeps your veggies off the heated bottom of your pressure cooker. The steamer handles can be used to lift items easily from your pressure cooker. It also works great in your microwave. It can be used to lift a whole chicken out of your Instant Pot without the chicken falling apart.

4. **7-inch Spring Form Non-Stick Pan:**

The spring form pan can be used for baking. It can be used for baking cakes, cheesecakes, and bread. These sizes will fit into your pressure cooker 5, 6, 8 quarts.

5. **Cook's Stainless-Steel Steamer Basket / Colander:**

Most pressure cookers don't come with this basket! These tool helps to keep your food items off the bottom of the pressure cooker and out of the water. Food items such as pasta do not require draining when cooking in a pressure cooker but having the pasta in this basket helps to easily lift the pasta from the pressure cooker.

6. **Clear lid:**

The clear lid comes with a steam vent and handle. It is used for sautéing or slow-cooking. It comes in different sizes such as 3, 6, and 8-quart sizes.

7. **Extra Silicone Rings:**

The extra silicone rings are needed on hand at all times. It can be used to switch out rings depending on whether you're cooking a sweet or savory dish. They usually wear out after multiple uses, but it's advisable to have an extra at hand.

8. **Steaming Rack:**

The steaming rack can be used to steam your veggies, pot-stickers and proteins in your pressure cooker.

9. **Mesh steaming basket:**

This is another helpful variation of a steamer. The mesh steaming basket can be used for steaming, frying and straining in your pressure cooker. It can be used for multiple purposes.

10. **Extra Stainless Steel:**

It makes it easier to prepare multiple dishes. You just have to switch out the pots rather than cleaning one over and over again.

11. **Cheesecake pan:**

The cheesecake pan can be used for making cheesecake in your Instant Pot. The bottom is removable but doesn't leak and can be used for dessert after steaming all the veggies.

12. **Instant Read Digital Meat Thermometer:**

This thermometer can be used for measuring the heat content in your meat while pressure cooking. Having the Meat Thermometer on hand puts an end to serving undercooked or over cooked meat. The meat thermometer can also be used for daily cooking or grilling.

It is important to clean your Instant Pot right after dinner or right after you're done using it, because:

- The spills, drips, etc. are still warm and clean up more easily when cleaning right away.
- You'll appreciate your Instant Pot being clean the next time you're ready to use it.

What NOT to do when cleaning your Instant Pot:

Ensure that you clean your Instant Pot right after cook and avoid the following practices when cleaning:

- Do not submerge the base of your Instant Pot in water.
- Do not leave it plugged in while cleaning it.

Tools you will need when cleaning your Instant Pot include:

- Washcloth
- Non-scratch scouring pad
- Towel
- Dish soap or all-purpose spray cleaner
- Vinegar
- Baking soda
- Toothbrush or any other small cleaning brushes

How to Clean Your Instant Pot:

1. Fill your sink with hot and soapy water. This step is the most important because it will make the cleaning easier and faster.

2. Always ensure that you unplug your Instant Pot and remove the insert pot from the base of your Instant Pot.

3. Place every accessory that requires cleaning in the hot, soapy water. Dump out any liquid that must have accumulated in the condensation cup. Place the silicone ring, valve cover if your model has a removable valve cover, sealing valve, and lid in the soapy water.

4. Dip a small toothbrush or cleaning brush in the hot, soapy water. Use the small brush to clean all the nooks and crannies of the base. Make use of a wet, wrung-out cloth in sopping up any liquids or dislodged food particles in your Instant Pot. The toothbrush and washcloth can be used to reach and dislodge any stuck food particles.

5.   Use a washcloth and all-purpose spray cleaner to wipe down the outside of your Instant Pot to look pretty and shiny.

6.   Wash the accessories that's been soaking in the hot, soapy water. After washing, rinse and air dry with the towel.

7.   Make use of the toothbrush to scrub the silicone ring. Use baking soda to remove any odor and staining. You can soak the silicon ring in vinegar water for a few hours. Rinse and air dry after washing.

8.   Scrub the inside of the insert pot in circular motion with non-scratch scouring pad. Make use of baking soda for stubborn messes.

9.   Scrub the following accessories with a small toothbrush — the lid, sealing valve, condensation cup and wipe with a towel to dry.

The answers to Frequently Asked Questions before purchasing an Instant Pot are listed below:

1. What is an Instant Pot? Is it the same as a pressure cooker?

Yes, the Instant Pot is the same as the pressure cooker and is currently one of the most popular electric pressure cooker models. It is a multi-functional cooker and has some extra functions such as rice cooker, soup, poultry, meat, yogurt, sauté pan etc.

2. Does the Instant Pot really speed up the cooking process?

Pressure cooking is always faster and saves time and energy. The fast cooking process of the pressure cooker may not be noticeable for some foods like broccoli or shrimps. Foods such as pulled pork can be cooked in less than 90 minutes, while it usually takes about 2 to 4 hours to make in the oven.

3. Are there any disadvantages with cooking in the Instant Pot?

The disadvantage of pressure cooking with pressure cookers is that you can't inspect, taste, or adjust the food along the way the cooking cycle. That's why it's necessary to follow the exact recipes instructions with accurate cooking times.

4. Is Instant Pot safe to use?

Most modern electric pressure cookers like the Instant Pot are quiet, very safe and easy to use. The Instant Pot has about 10 different safety mechanisms to avoid some of the potential issues. It has lots of safety features to prevent potential issues.

5. What is Instant Pot's working pressure?

The Instant Pot working pressure is within the range of 10.15~11.6 psi.

6. Can Instant Pot be used for Pressure Canning?

No, the Instant Pot has not been tested for food safety in pressure canning. The cooking features in Instant Pot IP-CSG, IP-LUX and IP-DUO series are regulated by a pressure sensor instead of a thermometer. Hence, the elevation of your location can disrupt the actual cooking temperature. For that very reason, it is not advisable to use your Instant Pot for pressure canning purpose.

7. Can I use the Instant Pot for Pressure Frying?

We would not recommend pressure frying in any electric pressure cookers. The pressure cooker gasket may be melted by the splattering of hot frying oil.

1. What kind of Instant Pot accessories do you recommend?

There is hand-picked list of accessories we would recommend. The accessories include steamer baskets, meat thermometers, silicon egg mold, cheesecake pan, steaming rack etc.

2. What kind of accessories or containers can I use in the Instant Pot?

Any oven-safe accessories and containers can be used in your Instant Pot. Always have in mind that different materials will conduct heat differently and this will make the cooking times to vary. Always use stainless steel containers as because they easily conduct heat.

3. I just got my Instant Pot. What should I do first?

Congratulations and welcome to the party! Conduct an initial test run before cooking with your Instant Pot.

4. How to do a Quick Release?

When the cooking cycle is up, carefully move the venting knob from sealing position to venting position. It usually takes a few minutes and rapidly releases the pressure in the pressure cooker. Exercise some patient and wait until the floating valve completely drops before opening the lid.

5. How to do a Natural Release?

When the cooking cycle is up, you have to wait until the floating valve completely drops before opening the lid. Carefully turn the venting knob from sealing position to venting position. It will enable all the pressure to release before opening the lid. Natural pressure release usually takes about 10 – 25 minutes.

Breakfast Casserole

Preparation time: 10 minutes

Cooking time: 15 minutes

Total time: 25 minutes

Serves: 5

Ingredients:

- 1 ½ cups of quinoa, soaked in water for about an hour
- 1 ½ cups of water
- 1 tsp. ground cinnamon
- ¼ tsp. salt
- 1 (15 oz) can coconut milk, or any available milk
- 2 tsp. vanilla extract
- ¼ cup pure maple syrup

Optional Ingredients: Hemp hearts, fresh fruit, non-diary milk or coconut flakes

Cooking Instructions:

1. Soak the quinoa for an hour, drain and rinse well.

2. Mix together cinnamon, water, coconut milk, maple syrup, salt and vanilla along with quinoa in the bowl of your Instant Pot.

3. Close and lock the lid in place and ensure that the valve is in sealing position

4. Press the manual function to cook on low pressure for about 13 minutes.

5. When the time is up, use a natural pressure release for about 12 minutes.

6. Carefully open the lid and remove the pan from your Instant Pot.

7. Using 5 different bowls, add 1 cup of the quinoa with lids in each of the bowls and store them in the fridge

8. Serve and enjoy with optional ingredients like hemp hearts, fresh fruit, non-diary milk or coconut flakes.

Egg Muffins Breakfast

Preparation time: 10 minutes

Cooking time: 15 minutes

Total time: 25 minutes

Servings: 5

Ingredients:

- Cooking spray (Non spray)
- 7 large eggs
- ¼ tsp. salt
- 2 sliced scallions white and green parts
- ¼ cup of 55ml milk
- ⅓ cup of 28g shredded Parmesan cheese
- 1 cup of (30 g) fresh baby spinach, chopped
- ½ cup of (90 g) diced seeded tomato
- 2 sliced scallions white and green parts

Cooking Instructions:

1. Spray 6 oz ovenproof custard cups with nonstick cooking spray.

2. Whisk the eggs, milk, salt, and pepper until well blended as desired using a large bowl.

3. Equally divide the spinach, tomato, and scallions into custard cups. Take the egg mixture and pure over the veggies and Sporadically Sprinkle the Parmesan.

4. Pour 1 cup of water (225ml) into the instant pot and place a trivet in the bottom.

5. Take 4 out of the 8 custard cups and keep them on the trivet and also take another trivet and keep on top. Take also the remaining 4 custard cups and keep on it.

6. Close and lock the lid in place and ensure that the valve is in sealing position. Press the manual function to cook on low pressure for about 6 minutes.

7. When the time is up, use a natural pressure release for about 6 minutes. Carefully open the lid when the valve drops and carefully remove the cups.

8. Serve and enjoy the delicacy.

Creamy Taste Pumpkin Maple Oat

Preparation time: 7 minutes

Cooking time: 15 minutes

Total time: 22 minutes

Servings: 6

Ingredients:

- 1 cup of steel cut oats (gluten-free)
- 1 1/3 cups of water
- ½ tsp. salt
- 1 tsp. vanilla
- 1/3 cup of pumpkin
- 4 tsp. maple syrup
- 1/3 tsp. cinnamon
- 1 13oz can coconut milk
- 1 tsp. coconut sugar

Cooking Instructions:

1. Add the oats, coconut milk, water, salt and vanilla into Instant Pot.

2. Close and lock the lid in place and ensure that the valve is in sealing position

3. Press the manual function to cook on high pressure for about 12 minutes.

4. When the time is up, use a natural pressure release for about 10 minutes.

5. Add maple syrup, coconut sugar, cinnamon and pumpkin.

6. Your creamy taste pumpkin maple oat is ready.

7. Serve and Enjoy.

Spiced Pumpkin Apple Butter

Preparation time: 7 minutes

Cooking time: 13 minutes

Total time: 20 minutes

Yield: 5-6 Cups

Servings: 4

Ingredients:

- 1 tbsp. spice of pumpkin pie
- 2 cans pumpkin puree (17oz each)
- Fingertip of salt
- 5 apples, peeled and sliced into tiny pieces
- 1 bottle of hard apple cider (14oz)
- 1 cup of white sugar
- ¼ cup honey

Cooking Instructions:

1. In a medium bowl, whisk together all your ingredients until it blends.

2. Close and lock the lid in place and ensure that the valve is in sealing position

3. Press the manual button to cook on high pressure for about 13 minutes.

4. When the time is up, use a natural pressure release for about 15 minutes.

5. Carefully open the lid once the pressure has been released.

6. Take out your butter and allow it cool completely then get some containers, put the butter according to your desired quantity and put them in your refrigerator.

7. Serve and enjoy with family and friends.

Hard-Boiled Eggs

Preparation time: 6 minutes

Cooking time: 7 minutes

Total time: 13 minutes

Servings: 5

Ingredients:

- 5 large eggs
- 1 cup of water

Cooking Instructions:

1. Put the eggs on the rack and pour some water in the pot.

2. Add the steamer rack with eggs into the bottom of your Instant Pot.

3. Close and lock the lid in place and ensure that the valve is in sealing position

4. Press the manual key to cook on high pressure for about 5 minutes.

5. When the time is up, use a natural pressure release for about 5 minutes.

6. Carefully remove the eggs, put in cold water and peel it when it is cool.

7. Serve and enjoy!!!

Pepper Frittata & Broccoli Ham

Preparation time: 15 minutes

Cooking time: 40 minutes

Total time: 55 minutes

Servings: 6

Calories: 435 kcal

Ingredients:

- 2 cups of frozen broccoli
- 6oz ham cubed
- 1 cup of sliced sweet peppers
- 2 tsp. ground pepper
- 6 eggs
- 1 cup of sliced cheddar cheese
- 1 tsp. salt
- 1 cup of half and half

Cooking Instructions:

1. Get a 6 x 3 pan and used a silicone brush to get oil or butter all over the pan.

2. Arrange the sliced sweet peppers in the bottom of the pan and place the cubed ham on top of it and cover with frozen broccoli.

3. In a medium bowl, whisk together the eggs, half and half, salt, and pepper. Stir in shredded cheese.

4. Pour the egg mixture on top of your vegetables and ham and cover with foil or a silicone lid.

5. In the inner liner of your Instant Pot, place 2 cups of water.

8. Close and lock the lid in place and ensure that the valve is in sealing position.

9. Press the manual function to cook on high pressure for about 25 minutes.

6. When the time is up, use a natural pressure release for about 10 minutes.

7. Gently use a knife to loosen the sides of your frittata. Place a plate on top of the pan, and thump out the frittata onto the plate to your desired side facing up.

8. Serve and enjoy!

Regular Oatmeal

Preparation time: 6 minutes

Cooking time: 7 minutes

Total time: 13 minutes

Servings: 5

Ingredients:

- 1 cup of regular oats
- 3 cups of water or depending on your desired thickness of your Oatmeal.

Optional Toppings: apples, blueberries, strawberries, bananas, pears, sliced dates, cinnamon, flax seed, flax seed, maple syrup or agave, all kinds of nuts, coconut flakes, or peanut butter etc.

Cooking Instructions:

1. Put water and regular oats into the Instant Pot.

2. Close and lock the lid in place and ensure that the valve is in sealing position.

3. Press the manual setting to cook on high pressure for about 7 minutes.

4. When the time is up, use a natural pressure release for about 10 minutes.

5. Carefully open the lid once the pressure has been released.

6. Put the oatmeal into a bowl and add any optional toppings.

7. Serve and enjoy!!!

Breakfast Quinoa

Preparation time: 20 minutes

Cooking time: 5 minutes

Total time: 25 minutes

Servings: 5

Ingredients:

- 2 cups of well rinsed uncooked quinoa
- ½ tsp. vanilla
- 3 cups of water
- fingertip of salt
- 2 tbsp. maple syrup
- ⅓ tsp. ground cinnamon

Optional Toppings: milk, fresh berries, sliced almonds

Cooking Instructions:

1. Mix quinoa with water, maple syrup, vanilla, cinnamon, and salt into the Instant Pot.
2. Close and lock the lid in place and ensure that the valve is in sealing position.

3. Press the manual function to cook on high pressure for about 5 minutes.

4. When the time is up, use a natural pressure release for about 10 minutes.

5. Carefully open the lid turning it away from you to allow steam to disperse.

6. Put the hot quinoa in a plate and top with milk, berries, and sliced almonds.

7. Serve and enjoy!!!

Buckwheat Porridge

Preparation time: 8 minutes

Cooking time: 30 minutes

Total time: 38 minutes

Servings: 6

Ingredients:

- 1 cup of raw buckwheat
- 3 cups of rice milk
- 1 sliced banana
- ¼ cup of raisins
- 1 tsp. ground cinnamon
- ½ tsp. vanilla

Cooking Instructions:

1. Rinse buckwheat well and put in Instant Pot.

2. Put all the ingredients.

3. Close and lock the lid in place and ensure that the valve is in sealing position.

4. Press the manual key to cook on high pressure for about 6 minutes.

5. When the time is up, use a natural pressure release for about 20 minutes.

6. Carefully open lid and stir porridge with a long handled spoon.

7. Serve and enjoy.

Blueberry Breakfast

Preparation time: 5 minutes

Cooking time: 6 minutes

Total time: 11 minutes

Servings: 6

Ingredients:

- ⅓ cup of old fashioned oats
- ¼ cup of unsweetened almond milk
- ⅓ cup of fat free Greek yogurt
- ¼ cup of blueberries, fresh or frozen
- 1 tbsp. sweetener
- splash of vanilla
- 1 ½ cups of water
- fingertip of salt
- splash of cinnamon
- 1 tbsp. chia seeds

Cooking Instructions:

1. Add water into your empty pot

2. Using a pint size jar, add all ingredients.

3. Close top of jar with a piece of aluminum foil and place in the Instant Pot.

4. Close and lock the lid in place and ensure that the valve is in sealing position.

5. Press the manual function to cook on high pressure for about 6 minutes.

6. When the time is up, use a natural pressure release for about 7 minutes.

7. Carefully remove jar using a pot holder and set it on the counter to cool for some few minutes.

8. Serve and enjoy!

Chicken Tortilla Soup

Preparation time: 13 minutes

Cooking time: 5 minutes

Total time: 28 minutes

Servings: 7

Ingredients:

- 1 cup of black beans (salt less), drained and well rinsed
- 1 1/3 lb raw chicken breasts (boneless skinless)
- 13 oz. chopped tomatoes with green chilies
- 15 oz. chopped tomatoes (salt less)
- 1 cup of frozen corn dissolved
- 1 jalapeno chopped
- 2 cloves garlic finely chopped
- 1 tsp. ground cumin
- 1/3 tsp. black pepper
- 1 tsp. chili powder
- 1 medium onion chopped
- 1 tsp. Himalayan salt
- 5 cups of organic chicken stock, low sodium

Tortilla Strips:

- Olive oil cooking spray
- 6 organic corn tortillas
- Himalayan salt

Optional toppings: Avocado, cheese, lime, Greek yogurt, cilantro

Cooking Instructions:

1. Put all the ingredients for the soup into your Instant Pot and stir to mix properly.

2. Close and lock the lid in place and ensure that the valve is in sealing position. Press the manual setting to cook on high pressure for about 20 minutes.

3. When the time is up, use a natural pressure release for about 15 minutes. Carefully open the lid and shred the chicken with two forks.

4. Serve and enjoy with optional toppings!

Instant Pot Beef Stew

Preparation time: 13 minutes

Cooking time: 50 minutes

Total time: 1 hour and 3 minutes

Servings: 7

Ingredients:

Stew Ingredients:

- 10 oz whole mushrooms
- 2 cups of celery, cut into 1" pieces
- 1 big onion, halved, then chopped
- ½ cup of tomato juice
- ½ tsp. salt
- ¼ tsp. black pepper
- 2 lbs beef chuck roast, trimmed and chopped into 1" cubes
- 3 cups carrots, peeled and chopped into 1" pieces

Thickening Ingredients:

- 2 cups of tomato puree
- 1 tbsp. corn starch

Cooking Instructions:

1. Gather all of the stew ingredients into the Instant Pot.

2. Close and lock the lid in place and ensure that the valve is in sealing position.

3. Press the manual key to cook on high pressure for about 40 minutes.

4. When the time is up, use a natural pressure release for about 10 minutes.

5. Carefully open the lid once the pressure has been released.

6. Serve and enjoy with family and friends

Stuffed Pepper Soup
Preparation time: 13 minutes

Cooking time: 10 minutes

Total time: 23 minutes

Servings: 7

Ingredients:

- 1 cup cooked brown or white rice
- 1 ½ lbs Extra Lean Ground Turkey
- 15 oz. can Tomato Sauce
- 2 cups of chopped Green and Red Peppers
- 1 cup of Onion, chopped
- 4 cups of Beef Broth
- ½ tsp. Basil
- 2 packets of Chili Seasoning
- 13 oz. can chopped Tomatoes with Roasted Garlic and Onions

Cooking Instructions:

1. Sauté the meat and onion, put peppers, tomatoes and tomato sauce, broth, and spices.

2. Close and lock the lid in place and ensure that the valve is in sealing position.

3. Press the manual function to cook on high pressure for about 8 minutes.

4. When the time is up, use a natural pressure release for about 15 minutes.

5. Carefully open the lid once the pressure has been released.

6. Serve and enjoy!!!

Turkey Chili

Preparation time: 13 minutes

Cooking time: 4 hour 10 minutes

Total time: 4 hours 23 minutes

Servings: 5

Ingredients:

- 2 cups of chicken broth
- 2 tbsp. olive oil
- 1 Onion, chopped
- 2 15 oz cans diced tomatoes
- 3 cloves of garlic, minced
- 2 lbs lean ground turkey
- 2 cups of prepared Great Navy beans
- 1 4 oz can of green chili
- 1 ½ tbsp. cumin
- 1 tbsp. chili powder
- salt and pepper to taste
- 1 small butternut squash, peeled and chopped into tiny sizes

Optional Ingredients: cilantro and plain Greek yogurt all for garnish

Cooking Instructions:

1. Set Instant Pot to the Sauté feature.

2. Put olive oil and onions and sauté for about 4 minutes.

3. Put garlic and stir until desired fragrance, about 30 seconds. Put ground turkey and brown until well cooked.

4. Put chicken broth, beans, tomatoes, squash, chili, cumin, chili powder, salt & pepper. Stir to mix well.

5. Close and lock the lid in place and ensure that the valve is in sealing position. Press the manual function to cook on High Pressure for about 4 hour's 10 minutes.

6. When the time is up, use a natural pressure release for about 13 minutes.

5. Serve with optional toppings and enjoy.

Italian Wedding Soup

Preparation time: 7 minutes

Cooking time: 10 minutes

Total time: 17 minutes

Servings: 5

Ingredients:

- Parmesan Cheese
- Small Meatballs
- 5 cups of chicken stock
- 1 tsp of olive oil
- 1 ½ cup of spinach
- 1 cup of diced carrots
- 1/3 onion, chopped

Cooking Instructions:

1. Set Instant Pot to sauté feature and allow it heat up.

2. Put 1 tsp olive oil, onions and carrots and sauté for sometimes.

3. Put chicken stock, meatballs.

4 Close and lock the lid in place and ensure that the valve is in sealing position.

5 Press the manual button to cook on high pressure for about 10 minutes.

6 When the time is up, use a natural pressure release for about 13 minutes.

7 Serve with Parmesan cheese.

Beanless Beef Chili

Preparation time: 8 minutes

Cooking time: 25 minutes

Total time: 33 minutes

Servings: 5

Ingredients:

- 1 ½ cups of chopped carrots
- 2 cloves chopped garlic
- 1 tsp. salt
- 1 big onion, diced
- ½ cup of chopped celery
- 2 1/2 small cans of tomatoes with green chilies
- 1 cup of bell peppers, diced
- 1½ Lbs. ground beef
- 1 1/2 cups of zucchini, cut into half moons
- 2 tbsp. chili powder
- 1 tbsp. olive oil
- 1 tsp. ground cumin
- 1 tsp. oregano
- ¼ tsp. cayenne pepper
- 14 oz can tomato puree or tomato sauce

Cooking Instructions:

1. Set your Instant Pot to sauté feature and brown beef until it is well cooked.

2. Put garlic for the last minute to drain excess fat. You can set this aside.

3. Open the Instant pot and put oil, onions, celery, carrots, peppers and sauté until onions are fatigued.

4. Put zucchini, tomatoes, cooked beef, and sauce into the Instant Pot and stir.

5. Close and lock the lid in place and ensure that the valve is in sealing position.

6. Press the manual button to cook on high pressure for about 25 minutes.

7. When the time is up, use a natural pressure release for about 10 minutes.

8. Carefully open the lid once the pressure has been released. Add toppings of your choice like avocado or cilantro.

9. Serve and enjoy!!!

Italian Sausage Stew

Preparation time: 8 minutes

Cooking time: 10 minutes

Total time: 18 minutes

Servings: 4

Ingredients:

- ⅓ tsp. cumin
- 2 tbsp. butter to cook in
- ½ tsp. marjoram
- ¼ lb pastured ground pork
- ½ tsp. onion powder
- ½ tsp. garlic powder
- 1¼ tsp. basil
- Sea salt/pepper to taste
- ½ tsp. thyme
- 9 oz gluten free noodles
- ¼ tsp. cayenne
- 1 tsp. sea salt
- ¼ tsp. black pepper
- 1 medium onion, diced
- 3 carrots, diced
- 2 stalks of celery, diced
- 4 ½ cloves of garlic, finely chopped
- ½ cup of white wine
- Freshly grated pram, to garnish
- 17 oz can organic minced tomatoes
- 2 quarts bone broth
- 3 big handfuls chopped kale

Cooking Instructions:

1. Keep the Instant Pot on Sauté feature and warm it.

2. Put butter, pork and all of the seasonings. Stir to combine and brown the meat.

3. Put the onion, carrot, celery, and garlic, mix and cook for 5-7 minutes until the meats are soft and sweet.

4. Put the white wine to detach the pan scraping up any bits at the bottom.

5. Put the minced tomatoes, broth, kale and noodles and stir to mix properly.

7 Close and lock the lid in place and ensure that the valve is in sealing position.

8 Press the manual function to cook on high pressure for about 5 minutes.

9 When the time is up, use a natural pressure release for about 8 minutes.

6. Season with salt and pepper to taste.

7. Serve with freshly grated parmesan and enjoy.

Broccoli Cheese Soup
Preparation time: 7 minutes

Cooking time: 5 minutes

Total time: 12 minutes

Servings: 4

Ingredients:

- 2 tsp. butter
- 1 medium onion, chopped
- 1 1/3 cups of sharp cheddar cheese
- 1 cup chopped carrots
- 4 cups of broccoli, roughly chopped (about 1/2 lb)
- 2 cups of cauliflower, diced (about 6 oz)
- ½ tsp. salt & pepper, to taste
- 2 cups broccoli, chopped into small pieces (1/4 lbs)
- 5 cups low-sodium chicken broth (1 (32 oz)

Cooking Instructions:

1. Set the Instant Pot to sauté function, put the butter in your pot to melt and put the onions/carrots in the butter until they start to soften.

2. Put the roughly chopped broccoli. Note, you don't need to add the broccoli that you chopped into small pieces yet.

3. Put the cauliflower, 1/2 tsp salt and the broth. Keep the lid on and set on manual for 3 minutes, quick release when it's finished.

4. If you have a regular blender, blend in batches everything inside the pot. You can now put the finely chopped broccoli.

5. Close and lock the lid in place and ensure that the valve is in sealing position. Press the manual function to cook on high pressure for about 10 minutes.

6. When the time is up, use a natural pressure release for about 8 minutes. Carefully open the lid and remove the pan from your Instant Pot. Stir in the cheese, and put pepper to your desired taste.

11. Serve and enjoy!!!

Loaded Potato & Cauliflower Soup
Preparation time: 8 minutes

Cooking time: 8 minutes

Total time: 16 minutes

Servings: 4

Ingredients:

- 5 cups of low-sodium chicken broth
- 1 1/4 cups sliced leeks
- 3 cloves garlic, diced
- 3 sliced scallions
- 3 1/2 cups of Yukon gold potatoes, peeled and diced
- 4 ½ cups of chopped cauliflower florets
- 1/3 cup of coconut milk (optional)
- 1 tsp. olive oil and 1 tsp butter
- ¼ tsp. fresh ground black pepper
- 1 package of all-natural, nitrite-free turkey bacon cooked and minced
- Shredded cheddar cheese

Cooking Instructions:

1. Set Instant Pot to sauté mode and spray with cooking oil spray.

2. Sauté diced bacon, and then remove from pot.

3. Put in olive oil and butter, sauté the leeks and garlic.

4. Put cauliflower, potatoes, salt and stock.

7. Close and lock the lid in place and ensure that the valve is in sealing position.

8. Press the manual key to cook on high pressure for about 10 minutes.

5. Use an immersion blender to blend everything and put coconut milk, if desired, then top with cheese, bacon.

6. Serve and enjoy with love ones!

Spicy Sweet Potato Chili

Preparation time: 8 minutes

Cooking time: 12 minutes

Total time: 20 minutes

Calories: 335 kcal

Servings: 4

Ingredients:

- 1 can black beans drained
- 1 cup celery stalks, chopped
- 1 peeled and chopped sweet potato
- 1 big onion chopped
- 1 cup of bell pepper
- 1 tsp. cayenne peppers
- ½ cup of crushed tomatoes
- 2 cups of chicken stock
- 1 Lb ground turkey
- 1 tsp. cumin
- 2 chipotle peppers in adobo sauce
- 1 tbsp. diced garlic

Cooking Instructions:

1. Using sauté function, sauté ground turkey and remove the grease from the pot.

2. Put garlic and onions and cook.

3. Combine cumin and cayenne pepper and add chipotle peppers, black beans, crushed tomatoes, sweet potatoes, and chicken stock.

4. Stir properly until everything is mixed.

5. Close and lock the lid in place and ensure that the valve is in sealing position.

6. Press the manual function to cook on high pressure for about 15 minutes.

7. When the time is up, use a natural pressure release for about 12 minutes.

8. Carefully open the lid and switch Instant Pot to sauté mode.

9   Put your bell peppers and celery. Allow for about 8 minutes until the celery is well cooked.

10 Switch off Instant Pot and Top with cheese, cilantro, and avocado.

11 Serve and enjoy!!!

Red Wine Beef Stew

Preparation time: 25 minutes

Cooking time: 1 hour 15 minutes

Total time: 1 hour 40 minutes

Calories: 550 kcal

Servings: 5

Ingredients:

- 3 lbs. boneless beef chuck cut into small pieces
- 3 tbsp. olive oil
- 1 tsp. corn starch
- 1 ¹/² cups of pearl onions frozen, dissolved
- 1 Lb. carrots cut into 2-inch sections
- 4 inch rosemary sprig
- 5 inch thyme sprig
- 1 tsp. sale
- 1 tsp. black pepper
- 1 ¹/³ cups of red wine a big red, like a Syrah
- 5 dried figs stemmed

Cooking Instructions:

1. Set the Instant pot on sauté feature and heat the olive oil.

2. Put the boneless beef, turn continuously for about 5 minutes and turn it into a large bowl.

3. Put onions and cook for about 7 minutes. Put wine and stir, remove any browned bits on the bottom of the pan.

4. Put carrots, figs, rosemary, thyme, salt and pepper. Put the beef back to the pan.

5. Close and lock the lid in place and ensure that the valve is in sealing position.

9. Press the manual setting to cook on high pressure for about 35 minutes.

10. When the time is up, use a natural pressure release for about 25 minutes.

11. Carefully open the lid and remove the thyme and rosemary.

12 In a small bowl, whisk the cornstarch with 2 tsp water and Stir this into the pot, until thickened.

13 Top with rice, noodles, or steamed potatoes.

14 Serve and enjoy!!!

Lemon Chicken Noodle Soup
Preparation time: 10 minutes

Cooking time: 25 minutes

Total time: 35 minutes

Ingredients:

- 1 cup of chopped fresh flat-leaf parsley
- 1 $^{1/2}$ cup of chopped celery
- 1 tsp. salt, divided pepper, to taste
- 2 cloves of garlic, diced
- 2 big chicken breasts, trimmed (about 1 1/2 lbs total)
- 3 cups of chopped carrots
- 4 cups of low-sodium chicken broth (38 oz)
- 3 cups of dry whole wheat egg noodles
- 2 lemons, zested and juiced (about 1/4 cup of lemon juice)
- 1 tsp. dried thyme
- 1 tsp. herbes d' provence
- 1 bundle green onions, whites and greens separated and chopped (about 1 cup, chopped)

Cooking Instructions:

1. Put olive oil or coconut oil into your Instant Pot.

2. Switch on the sauté function and fry the whites of the onions, celery and carrots, season with salt and pepper to taste, until the carrots start to brown a bit.

3. Put the diced garlic and cook for sometimes. Put the broth, chicken breasts to the pot, making sure that your chicken is completely covered by the broth.

5 Close and lock the lid in place and ensure that the valve is in sealing position. Press the manual function to cook on high pressure for about 10 minutes.

6 When the time is up, use a natural pressure release for about 10 minutes. Carefully open the lid and remove the pan from your Instant Pot.

7 Put the dry pasta to the pot, put the lid back on setting it to "sealing" and set on manual for zero minutes.

8 While the pasta is cooking, shred the chicken with two forks. Switch off your pot when the pasta is done, and again do a quick release, take off the lid and add the shredded chicken back.

9 Put the lemon zest, lemon juice, thyme, herbes d' provence, parsley, the remaining green onions.

10 Serve and enjoy!!!

Chipotle Pumpkin Turkey Chili

Preparation time: 8 minutes

Cooking time: 15 minutes

Total time: 23 minutes

Servings: 4

Ingredients:

- 1 cup of chicken broth (low-sodium)
- 1 $^{1/2}$ red onion, chopped
- 1 big green bell chopped pepper
- 2 stalks of chopped celery
- 1 lb. lean ground turkey
- 1 tsp. cinnamon
- 2$^{1/2}$ tsp. cumin
- 1 tbsp. chili powder
- 2 tsp. chipotle puree
- Salt
- 1 can (14 1/2 oz) petite diced tomatoes
- 1 can (15 oz) pumpkin puree
- 1 can well rinsed and drained (15 oz) black beans
- 2 cloves of garlic, diced

Optional Toppings: Chopped cilantro and plain Greek yogurt

Cooking Instructions:

1. Set the Instant Pot to sauté mode, put the following on the pot - ground turkey and minced garlic salt and pepper.

2. Cook until the turkey turns brown. You may not completely cook the turkey because it'll later be cooked completely.

3. Put the peppers, onions and celery and cook one for sometimes while you sprinkle the cinnamon, cumin and chili powder.

5 Switch off the sauté mode, and then put the tomatoes and the broth. Close and lock the lid in place and ensure that the valve is in sealing position.

6 Press the manual function to cook on high pressure for about 7 minutes. Carefully open the lid and remove the pan from your Instant Pot.

7   Switch on the sauté mode back, put the drained beans, the pumpkin puree and the chipotle puree and then stir, tasting as you go so you get the spice level that you want.

8   Put a bit more cinnamon, cumin and chili powder. When the time is up, use a natural pressure release for about 10 minutes.

9   Use cilantro and plain Greek yogurt as your optional toppings.

10 Serve and enjoy!!!

13 Bean Soup
Preparation time: 6 minutes

Cooking time: 15 minutes

Total time: 21 minutes

Servings: 4

Ingredients:

- 1 cup of carrots chopped
- 1 ham bone
- 1 big diced tomato
- 2 cups of celery minced
- 2 tsp. chili powder
- 1 tsp. garlic powder
- 1 tsp. sea salt
- 1 big diced tomato
- 1 big diced tomato
- ¼ tsp. pepper
- 2 cups of 13 bean soup consisting of various beans, lentils, peas

Cooking Instructions:

1. Put your beans in the Instant Pot and put 3 ¹/² cups of water.

2. Close and lock the lid in place and ensure that the valve is in sealing position. Select Manual function to cook on High Pressure for 15 minutes.

3. When the time is up, use a natural pressure release for about 8-10 minutes. Carefully rinse and drain the beans, put the beans back into the Instant Pot and add the ham bone.

5 Put enough water and cook, setting the cooker with a natural pressure release. Remove the ham bone, add all the ingredients. Close and lock the lid in place and ensure that the valve is in sealing position.

6 Press the manual key to cook on high pressure for about 15 minutes. When the time is up, use a natural pressure release for about 20 minutes.

7 Serve and enjoy!!!

Rice & Beans

Preparation time: 6 minutes

Cooking time: 15 minutes

Total time: 21 minutes

Calories: 270 kcal

Servings: 6

Ingredients:

- 2 ¹/₂ cups of short grain brown rice
- 1 onion chopped
- 2 red peppers diced
- 1 tbsp. taco seasoning
- 1 cup dried red beans
- 1 cup salsa
- 2 cups of vegetable or chicken stock
- 1 tsp. diced garlic
- ½ tbsp. avocado oil

Optional Toppings: cheese, sour cream, cilantro

Cooking Instructions:

1. Switch Instant Pot to sauté mode on high pressure and allow to heat up.

2. Put oil, onions, peppers, garlic and fry for at least 3 minutes.

3. Put rice, beans, salsa, seasonings and stock, stir thoroughly.

4. Close and lock the lid in place and ensure that the valve is in sealing position

5. Press the manual key to cook on high pressure for about 21 minutes.

6. When the time is up, use a natural pressure release for about 15 minutes.

7. Carefully open the lid and remove the pan from your Instant Pot.

8. Serve with toppings of choice and enjoy!!!

Baked Beans

Preparation time: 7 minutes

Cooking time: 40 minutes

Total time: 47 minutes

Servings: 6

Cooking Ingredients:

- 3 cloves garlic, diced
- 1 tsp. sea salt
- 2 lbs. small white beans
- 1 tbsp. mustard powder
- 1 big onion, minced
- 1 cup molasses
- 1/2 cup of maple syrup
- ¼ tsp. ground pepper
- 5 cups of water
- 2 cups of balsamic vinegar

Cooking Instructions:

1. Put the beans with 2 or 3 cups water into the bottom of your Instant Pot and cook on high pressure for 10 minutes.

4 Rinse and drain the water out then place them back into the Instant Pot. Put enough water and put all the ingredients.

5 Close and lock the lid in place and ensure that the valve is in sealing position. Press the manual function to cook on high pressure for about 40 minutes.

6 When the time is up, use a natural pressure release for about 25 minutes. Cook on bean setting for 40 minutes and release natural pressure.

7 Carefully open the lid and remove the pan from your Instant Pot.

8 Serve and enjoy with friends and family.

Santa Fe Beans and Rice

Preparation time: 10 minutes

Cooking time: 25 minutes

Total time: 35 minutes

Servings: 5

Ingredients:

For the beans and rice:

- 1 (20 oz) can corn, rinsed and drained
- 2 cups of long grain brown rice
- 2 cups of water
- 1 (20 oz) can kidney beans, rinsed and drained
- 1 (10 oz) can tomato sauce
- 1 cup of picante sauce
- 1 tsp. salt
- 1/2 tsp. pepper
- 1 (20 oz) can black beans, rinsed and drained
- 2 tbsp. taco seasoning

Optional Toppings: 1 ½ lbs boneless, skinless chicken thighs or breasts, grated cheddar

For the garlic lime sour cream:

- 2 tsp. lime juice
- 1 tsp. lime zest
- 1 cup sour cream
- 2 garlic cloves, diced
- 2 cups of chopped cilantro
- 1 tsp. kosher salt

Cooking Instructions:

1. Put rice and water into the Instant pot.

2. Without stirring, put the kidney beans, black beans, corn, tomato sauce, picante sauce, taco seasoning, salt and pepper on top.

3 Close and lock the lid in place and ensure that the valve is in sealing position. Press the manual function to cook on high pressure for about 25 minutes.

4   When the time is up, use a natural pressure release for about 7 minutes.

5   Prepare the garlic lime sour cream by mixing together sour cream, cilantro, lime zest, lime juice, kosher salt and garlic cloves.

6   Scoop rice and beans into a plate with a dollop of the sour cream on top with a little topping of grated cheddar, if desired.

7   Serve and enjoy!!!

Pinto Beans

Preparation time: 5 minutes

Cooking time: 1 hour 25 minutes

Total time: 1 hour 30 minutes

Calories: 180 kcal

Servings: 5

Ingredients:

- 5 cups of water
- 1 lb. dry pinto beans
- salt and pepper to taste
- 1 tbsp. Better Than Bullion vegetable base

Cooking Instructions:

1. Wash and drain your pinto beans using a wire mesh strainer.

2. Put them back into the Instant Pot with water and better than Bullion vegetable base.

3. Close and lock the lid in place and ensure that the valve is in sealing position.

4. Press the manual key to cook on high pressure for about 1 hour 25 minutes.

5. When the time is up, use a natural pressure release for about 20 minutes.

6. Carefully open the lid once the pressure has been released.

7. Serve and enjoy!!!

Refried Beans

Preparation time: 5 minutes

Cooking time: 30 minutes

Total time: 35 minutes

Servings: 5

Cooking Ingredients:

- 1 1/2 cup pinto beans, selected and washed
- 3 cups of filtered water
- 1 medium onion
- 1 jalapeno, diced
- 1 tbsp. sea salt
- ¼ cup avocado oil
- 1 bay leaf
- 2 cloves garlic, chopped

Cooking Instructions:

1. Put beans, water, bay leaf and garlic into the bottom of your Instant Pot.

2. Close and lock the lid in place and ensure that the valve is in sealing position.

3. Select Manual function to cook on high pressure for 30 minutes. When the time is up, use a natural pressure release.

4. Turn the beans and water into a big container and set the Instant Pot to sauté mode. Sauté the onion and jalapeno in the olive oil and put the sea salt.

5. Put the beans and water back into the Instant Pot using the same settings. Mix thoroughly the beans and cook until your refried beans are thickened.

6. When the time is up, use a natural pressure release for about 25 minutes. Carefully open the lid once the pressure has been released.

7. Serve and enjoy!!!

Chicken Taco Bowls

Preparation time: 5 minutes

Cooking time: 30 minutes

Total time: 35 minutes

Calories: 270 kcal

Servings: 7

Ingredients:

- 2 cups of long grain white rice , rinsed and drained
- 1 ½ cups low sodium chicken broth
- 1 ½ packet taco seasoning
- 1 oz can black beans , rinsed and drained
- 2 chicken breasts
- 1 ½ cups of salsa
- 1 cup of corn

Toppings: Sour cream, cheese, chopped cilantro, chopped green onion, sliced avocado

Cooking Instructions:

1. Fill instant pot with non-stick cooking spray. Add half cup chicken broth into the Instant Pot.

2. Put chicken breasts and stir chicken with taco seasoning. Add the black beans and corn. Add salsa.

3. Put rice and remaining 1 cup chicken broth. Place the rice into the liquid and stir thoroughly.

8 Close and lock the lid in place and ensure that the valve is in sealing position.

9 Press the manual function to cook on high pressure for about 8 minutes.

10 When the time is up, use a natural pressure release for about 10 minutes.

11 Carefully open the lid once the pressure has been released.

12 Slide rice to the side a bit to find the chicken breasts and pull them out.

13 Shred the chicken and put a scoop of rice mixture to a bowl.

14 Top with some chicken and other desired toppings.

15 Serve and enjoy!!!

Honey Garlic Chicken

Preparation time: 5 minutes

Cooking time: 30 minutes

Total time: 35 minutes

Calories: 340 kcal

Servings: 7

Ingredients:

- 1 tbsp. sesame seed oil
- ⅓ cup of honey
- 4 cloves garlic, minced
- salt and fresh ground pepper, to taste
- ½ cup of salt less ketchup
- ½ tsp. dried oregano
- 2 tbsp. chopped fresh parsley
- 6 bone-in, skinless chicken thighs
- ½ tbsp. toasted sesame seeds, for garnish
- sliced green onions
- ½ cup low sodium soy sauce

Cooking Instructions:

1. Get a container and carefully mix honey, minced garlic, soy sauce, ketchup, oregano and parsley and set aside.

2. Set the Instant Pot to sauté mode and heat the pot. Add sesame oil to the pot. Put chicken thighs with salt and pepper and cook for about 3 minutes per side.

3. Put already prepared honey-garlic sauce to the Instant Pot. Close and lock the lid in place and ensure that the valve is in sealing position.

4. Press the manual button to cook on high pressure for about 20 minutes. When the time is up, use a natural pressure release for about 10 minutes.

5. Carefully open the lid once the pressure has been released. Put the chicken on a serving plate and scoop the sauce over the chicken. You can garnish with toasted sesame seeds and green onions.

6. Serve and enjoy.

Buttery Lemon Chicken

Preparation time: 7 minutes

Cooking time: 10 minutes

Total time: 17 minutes

Servings: 5

Ingredients:

- 2 lbs. chicken breast or thighs
- 2 tbsp. ghee or butter
- 1 onion, diced
- 1 cup organic chicken broth
- 3 cloves diced garlic
- 1 tsp. salt
- 1 tsp. paprika
- ½ tsp. pepper
- 1 tsp. dried parsley
- ½ cup lemon juice, 2 lemons
- 3 tsp. arrowroot flour

Cooking Instructions

1. Put the Instant Pot on sauté mode and add butter to melt.

2. Put onion, garlic, paprika, parsley, and pepper and fry for about 2 -3 minutes.

3. Using the same setting put the chicken and fry until it becomes brownish. Put chicken brother, lemon juice, and salt over chicken and stir.

4. Close and lock the lid in place and ensure that the valve is in sealing position. Press the manual key to cook on high pressure for about 8 minutes.

5. When the time is up, use a natural pressure release for about 10 minutes. Remove the chicken from the Instant Pot, but leave the sauce in the pan.

6. Gently pour arrowroot flour to thicken the sauce.

7. Serve and enjoy!!

Kung Pao Chicken

Preparation time: 7 minutes

Cooking time: 25 minutes

Total time: 32 minutes

Calories: 1805 kcal

Servings: 5

Ingredients:

For the chicken:

- Green onion to garnish
- 1 zucchini minced
- 1/2 red bell pepper diced
- 1/2 cup of onion chopped red or white
- 3 1/2 garlic cloves diced
- 2 tbsp. vegetable oil
- 1 cup of cashews or peanuts
- 1 ½ lbs. Chicken skinless chicken breast

For the sauce:

- 1/4 tsp. ground black pepper
- 2/3 cup of garlic coconut amino
- 1/2 tsp. red pepper flakes
- 1/2 tsp. ground ginger

Cooking Instructions:

1. Put oil to Instant Pot and fry chicken until it gets brownish.

2. Put all vegetables and stir. Add sauces. Close and lock the lid in place and ensure that the valve is in sealing position.

3. Press the manual function to cook on low pressure for about 25 minutes.

4. When the time is up, use a natural pressure release for about 7 minutes.

5. Carefully remove the lid and give everything a good stir.

6. Serve and enjoy!!!

Preparation time: 7 minutes

Cooking time: 15 minutes

Total time: 22 minutes

Servings: 5

Ingredients:

- 5 chicken breasts (not thin breasts).
- ¾ cup of favorite dark sweet barbecue sauce
- 2 tbsp. soy sauce
- ¾ cup of orange marmalade
- 2 tsp. cornstarch
- chopped green onions for garnish

Cooking Instructions:

1. Carefully shred chicken breasts into small sizes.

2. Add the chopped chicken, barbecue sauce, and soy sauce into you're the bottom of your Instant Pot.

3. Close and lock the lid in place and ensure that the valve is in sealing position. Select manual function to cook on high pressure for 5 minutes.

4. When the time is up, use a natural pressure release for about 7 minutes.

5. Remove ¹/₃ cup of the barbecue chicken sauce from the Instant Pot and mix with cornstarch in a small bowl.

6. Put cornstarch broth mixture back into Instant Pot. Put orange marmalade and stir properly.

7. Close and lock the lid in place and ensure that the valve is in sealing position. Press the manual function to cook on high pressure for about 8 minutes.

8. When the time is up, use a natural pressure release for about 7 minutes. Carefully remove the lid and garnish with green onions.

9. Serve and enjoy with family!!!

Ground Turkey Lentil Chili

Preparation time: 25 minutes

Cooking time: 20 minutes

Total time: 45 minutes

Servings: 5

Ingredients:

- 1 (10 oz) can tomato sauce
- 2 lb. ground turkey
- 2 diced garlic cloves
- 2 tbsp. tomato paste
- 1/2 tsp. pepper
- 1 1/2 tsp. salt
- 1 1/2 cup of dry green lentils
- 2 cups of water
- 1 (12 oz) can petite diced tomatoes
- 1 (4 oz) can diced green chili
- 2 tsp. chili powder
- 1 tsp. cumin
- 1 medium yellow onion, diced

Cooking Instructions:

1. Switch your Instant Pot on to sauté. Fry the ground turkey to brown.

2. Put the minced onions, garlic, tomato paste and salt and cook until meat is browned and onions are soften.

3. Put the lentils, water, tomato sauce, diced tomatoes, green chili, chili powder, cumin and pepper.

4. Close and lock the lid in place and ensure that the valve is in sealing position.

5. Press the manual key to cook on high pressure for about 15 minutes. When the time is up, use a natural pressure release for about 15 minutes.

6. Carefully remove the lid and scoop the chili into plates. Top with a dollop of sour cream and some diced green onions.

7. Serve and enjoy!!!

Korean Chicken Meatballs

Preparation time: 5 minutes

Cooking time: 20 minutes

Total time: 25 minutes

Servings: 5

Ingredients:

- 2 egg
- 2 lb. ground chicken
- $1^{1/2}$ tsp. olive oil
- 2 garlic cloves, minced
- 1 tbsp. grated ginger (not packed)
- 1 tsp. red pepper flakes
- $1/2$ tbsp. sesame oil
- $1/2$ cup of panko crumbs
- $1/2$ cup of Korean BBQ Sauce
- $1/3$ tsp. salt

Cooking Instructions:

1. Mix all the ingredients together except for the panko crumbs, Korean BBQ sauce, and green onions.

2. Put the panko crumbs over the chicken, mix and let the panko soak into the chicken mixture for 7 minutes.

3. Make about 10 balls, put the olive oil to the bottom of the Instant Pot and then put the chicken to the Instant Pot.

4. Close and lock the lid in place and ensure that the valve is in sealing position.

5. Press the manual function to cook on high pressure for about 20 minutes.

6. When the time is up, use a natural pressure release for about 8 minutes.

7. Prepare the Korean BBQ Sauce while the balls are cooking.

8. Serve and enjoy!!!

Chicken and Dumplings

Preparation time: 5 minutes

Cooking time: 8 minutes

Total time: 13 minutes

Servings: 4

Ingredients:

- 2 cups of chicken broth
- 1 cup of water
- 1 tsp olive oil
- 1 ½ lbs chicken breast cubed
- 1 tube 16oz refrigerated biscuits
- 1 cup chopped carrots
- 1 cup of frozen peas
- 2 tsp. oregano
- 1 tsp. onion powder
- 1 tsp. basil
- 2 cloves minced garlic
- ½ tsp. salt
- ½ tsp. pepper

Cooking Instructions:

1. Slice each biscuit to about ¼ thickness. Using a knife, cut into half strips.

2. Put 1 ¹/² tsp olive oil into the instant pot, add also chicken, oregano, onion powder, basil, garlic, salt and pepper and mix to your desired coat.

3. Close and lock the lid in place and ensure that the valve is in sealing position

4. Press the manual function to cook on high pressure for about 8 minutes and stir at intervals until it becomes brownish.

5. After cooking time is up, switch off instant pot. Put 2 cups of chicken broth and 1 cup of water, carrots and peas to Instant Pot and stir properly until mixed and add biscuits.

6. Close and lock the lid in place and ensure that the valve is in sealing position. Press the manual function to cook on high pressure for about 5 minutes.

7. When the time is up, use a natural pressure release for about 5 minutes. Carefully open the lid once the pressure has been released.

8. Serve and enjoy!!!

Honey Lemon Chicken
Preparation time: 12 minutes

Cooking time: 35 minutes

Total time: 47 minutes

Calories: 370 kcal

Servings: 4

Ingredients:

- 3 cloves garlic, peeled and diced
- 1 lb. bone-in, skin-on chicken thighs
- 1 1/2 tsp lemon pepper seasoning
- zest of one lemon
- 3 tbsp. honey
- 2 1/2 tbsp. water
- 1 tbsp. soy sauce
- 1 tsp. corn starch
- 1/3 cup of freshly squeezed lemon juice (about 1 lemon)
- 1/3 cup of water
- 2 tbsp. canola oil
- Corn starch Slurry for thickening of the sauce

Cooking Instructions:

1. Trim the chicken thighs of excess fat and season with lemon pepper seasoning.

2. Set the Instant Pot on sauté mode. Put oil when the pot is hot and heat with the Instant Pot lid open.

3. Keep chicken in a single layer with skin side down. Cook for about 3 minutes and then turn the other side of the chicken to cook for another 3 minutes.

4. Remove surplus oil from the Instant Pot, put garlic and cook. Stir for about 20 to 30 seconds.

5. Using a small bowl, mix lemon juice, lemon zest, honey, water, and soy sauce. Stir properly until well mixed and pour over chicken.

6. Close and lock the lid in place and ensure that the valve is in sealing position. Press the manual button to cook on high pressure for about 15 minutes.

7. When the time is up, use a natural pressure release for about 7 minutes.

8. Carefully open the lid once the pressure has been released.

9. Serve and enjoy.

Chicken Tortilla-Less Soup

Preparation time: 7 minutes

Cooking time: 25 minutes

Total time: 32 minutes

Servings: 7

Ingredients:

For Soup:

- 1 tsp. dried oregano
- 1 tsp. onion powder
- 2 boneless skinless chicken breasts (about 1 lb)
- 2 cans ROTEL, any variety
- 2 tsp. adobe sauce
- 1 medium chopped onion
- 2 tsp. garlic powder
- 1 tsp. cumin
- 2 tsp. chili powder
- 1 tsp. smoked paprika
- 2 chipotle peppers in adobo sauce
- 1 ½ tsp. salt
- 2 zucchinis , chopped or cut into half inch moons
- 1 15 oz. can Whole30-compliant chicken broth
- 1 14 oz. can full-fat coconut milk or coconut cream , whisked until smooth

Garnishes: fresh avocado slices, red onions, sliced thin, fresh cilantro, and chopped coconut cream.

Cooking Instructions:

1. Pour salt on the boneless skinless chicken breasts.

2. Put the chicken breasts to the Instant Pot, put the remaining ingredients from ROTEL to medium onion, and put the spices and top with zucchini.

3. Close and lock the lid in place and ensure that the valve is in sealing position.

4. Press the manual function to cook on high pressure for about 20 minutes.

5. When the time is up, use a natural pressure release for about 12 minutes.

6. Carefully open the lid once the pressure has been released. Remove the chicken breasts and put coconut milk.

7. Turn Instant Pot to Sauté mode and stir to mix well. Dice chicken and return to soup.

8. Serve and enjoy!!!

Green Chili Chicken Enchilada Soup
Preparation time: 7 minutes

Cooking time: 25 minutes

Total time: 32 minutes

Servings: 7

Ingredients:

- 1 cup of thick and chunky salsa Verde
- 1 tbsp. cumin
- 2 ¹/² chicken breast halves (frozen or fresh)
- 4 ¹/² cups water
- 2 tsp. Better Than Bouillon Chicken Base
- 2 tbsp. lime juice
- 1 10 oz. can green chili enchilada sauce
- 1 5 oz. can green chili
- 1 ½ tsp. chili powder
- Salt and pepper
- 1 tsp. garlic powder
- ½ cup of long grain brown rice, uncooked
- 1 13 oz can seasoned white beans, drained
- 1 ½ cups of frozen sweet white corn
- 4 oz cream cheese
- 1 tsp. onion powder

Optional toppings: tortilla chips, grated cheese, sour cream, jalapenos, and cilantro

Cooking Instructions:

1. Put chicken, water, bouillon, enchilada sauce, green chili, salsa and cumin into the bottom of your Instant Pot.

2. Add the chili powder, onion powder, garlic powder, rice and beans to the Instant Pot. Give everything a good mix.

3. Close and lock the lid in place and ensure that the valve is in sealing position. Press the manual setting to cook on high pressure for about 25 minutes.

4. When the time is up, use a natural pressure release for about 15 minutes. Carefully open the lid. Place the chicken on a cutting board and shred.

5. Place them back to the pot. Sprinkle the corn and cream cheese until the cream cheese is melted.

6. Put the lime juice and stir. Add Salt and pepper to taste. Scoop into plates and add toppings of your choice.

7. Serve and enjoy!!!

Beef Stroganoff

Preparation time: 8 minutes

Cooking time: 25 minutes

Total time: 33 minutes

Calories: 321 kcal

Servings: 5

Ingredients:

- 1 tbsp. oil
- ½ cup of diced onions
- 1 tsp. pepper
- 1 tbsp. Worcestershire sauce
- 1 tsp. salt
- 1 lb. pork tips or beef stew meat
- ¾ cup of water
- 1 tbsp. garlic
- 1.5 cups of chopped mushrooms

For Finishing:

- ¼ cup sour cream
- 1/3 tsp xanthan gum (sub with arrowroot starch, corn starch or other thickener)

Cooking Instructions:

1. Switch Instant Pot on Sauté on high and put the oil, add onions and garlic when the oil is hot and stir for a while.

2. Put all ingredients except sour cream and close up the pot. Close and lock the lid in place and ensure that the valve is in sealing position

3. Press the manual key to cook on high pressure for about 8 minutes. When the time is up, use a natural pressure release for about 10 minutes. Open the Instant Pot, put sour cream and stir.

4. Pour the xanthan gum a little at a time, and keep stirring until the mix thickens. Scoop into plates and top some cauliflower rice or low carb noodles.

5. Serve and enjoy!!!

Pulled Pork

Preparation time: 30 minutes

Cooking time: 50 minutes

Total time: 1 hour 20 minutes

Calories: 421 kcal

Servings: 5

Ingredients:

- 2 chipotle peppers in adobo sauce, diced
- 5 lb. boneless pork loin or boneless pork shoulder/butt
- 1 tsp. kosher salt
- ½ tsp. black pepper
- BBQ. sauce (your favorite)
- 14 oz. Dr Pepper soda

Cooking Instructions:

1. Cut pork into 6 pieces and season with salt and pepper.

2. Put pork in instant pot insert and top with diced chipotle peppers and sprinkle Dr Pepper around the pork.

3. Close and lock the lid in place and ensure that the valve is in sealing position.

4. Press the manual mode to cook on high pressure for about 50 minutes.

5. When the time is up, use a natural pressure release for about 15 minutes.

6. Carefully open the lid once the pressure has been released.

7. Remove pork and put in a big bowl. Shred using two forks and add bbq sauce to your tastes.

8. Serve and enjoy!!!

Mongolian Beef

Preparation time: 15 minutes

Cooking time: 35 minutes

Total time: 50 minutes

Servings: 5

Ingredients:

- 8 cloves garlic , diced
- 1 tbsp. cornstarch
- 1 ¹/₂ tbsp extra virgin olive oil
- ½ cup of brown sugar
- ½ cup of lite soy sauce
- 1 lb flank steak, sliced across the grain
- 1 cup of water
- 1 tsp. red pepper flakes
- 1 tbsp. fresh ginger , diced

Cornstarch Slurry:

- 2 tbsp. cornstarch
- ½ cup of water

Garnish:

- ¹/₃ cup of green onions, chopped
- 1 tsp sesame seeds

Cooking Instructions:

1. Set the Instant Pot to Sauté mode. When it is hot, put sliced beef to a big bag that can be zipped and put 1 tbsp cornstarch and shake well to coat the beef properly.

2. Put the oil to the hot Instant Pot, once the oil is hot, add the beef and sauté for about 3 minutes and stir for sometimes.

3. Put the rest of the ingredients to the pot: minced garlic, ginger, lite soy sauce, brown sugar, water, red pepper flakes and stir properly until all the ingredients are mixed and coated in sauce.

4. Close and lock the lid in place and ensure that the valve is in sealing position. Press the manual function to cook on high pressure for about 10 minutes.

5. When the time is up, use a natural pressure release for about 10 minutes. Carefully open the lid and make the cornstarch slurry.

6. In medium bowl, mix cornstarch with water until fully mixed. Set the Instant Pot on the Sauté mode.

7. Add the cornstarch to the pot, stir to mix well and cook for 4 minutes stirring periodically, until the sauce thickens.

8. Switch off the Instant Pot and let the Mongolian Beef rest for 12 minutes so that the sauce will settle and thicken more.

9. Garnish with fresh chopped green onions and sesame seeds.

10. Serve and enjoy!!!

Spicy Thai Beef Nachos

Preparation time: 13 minutes

Cooking time: 9 minutes

Total time: 21 minutes

Servings: 5

Ingredients:

- 1 cup of Carrot, chopped
- 25 Scooped Corn Chips
- ½ cup of Cilantro, minced
- 1 ½ cups of Cheese, shredded
- ½ lb. Roast Beef, sliced or shredded
- 1 Shallot, minced
- ½ cup of Jarred Peanut Sauce
- Wedges of Lime for Spritzing
- Jarred Sliced Jalapenos
- 6 leaves Mint, diced

Cooking Instructions:

1. Spread Scooped corn chips and remove any broken chips.

2. Using a small container, mix sliced roast beef, carrot, shallot, mint, and cilantro. Spoon into chip cups. You may alternatively prepare like traditional nachos.

3. Top with shredded cheese and broil until cheese has melted and begins to bubble.

4. Take out from oven and drizzle with jarred peanut sauce, spritz with lime and top with sliced jalapeno if desired.

5. Serve immediately and enjoy.

Boneless Pork Chops

Preparation time: 6 minutes

Cooking time: 9 minutes

Total time: 15 minutes

Servings: 5

Ingredients:

- 1 stick of margarine
- boneless pork chops
- 1 package of ranch mix
- 1 1/2 cup of water
- 1 tbsp. of coconut oil

Cooking Instructions:

1. Put the pork chops in the Instant Pot and add a tbsp of coconut oil.

2. Switch on the sauté mode and fry to brown on both sides.

3. Put the margarine on top and stir in the ranch mix packet on top.

4. Put water over the pork and put the lid on and set to sealing.

5. Close and lock the lid in place and ensure that the valve is in sealing position.

6. Press the manual button to cook on high pressure for about 7 minutes.

7. When the time is up, use a natural pressure release for about 5 minutes.

8. Carefully open the lid once the pressure has been released.

9. Serve immediately and enjoy.

Korean Beef & Brown Rice

Preparation time: 10 minutes

Cooking time: 15 minutes

Total time: 25 minutes

Servings: 5

Ingredients:

For the rice:

- 1 tbsp. sesame oil
- 1 ½ cups of long grain brown rice
- 2 cups of water
- ½ tsp. salt

For the beef:

- ⅓ cup low sodium soy sauce
- 1 tsp. garlic powder
- ¼ tsp. ground red pepper
- 2 tsp. diced ginger
- ⅓ cup of brown sugar
- Toasted sesame seeds, for garnish
- 1 lb. lean ground beef
- Sliced green onions, for garnish
- 1 tbsp. tomato paste

Cooking Instructions:

1. Cover the bottom of the Instant Pot with non-stick cooking spray to help to stick rice and clean up. Put the rice, water, and salt in the bottom of the Instant Pot.

2. Using an oven safe dish that fits inside your Instant Pot stir together the brown sugar, soy sauce, sesame oil, garlic powder, red pepper, minced ginger and tomato paste.

3. Put the ground beef and break the beef up with a spoon. Stir the beef with the sauce to coat.

4. Keep the oven safe dish on top of the trivet as you lower the trivet and dish on top of the rice and water in the bottom of the Instant pot.

5. Close and lock the lid in place and ensure that the valve is in sealing position. Press the manual function to cook on high pressure for about 25 minutes.

6. When the time is up, use a natural pressure release for about 12 minutes. Remove the trivet and dish out of the Instant Pot.

7. If the bottom of the trivet is left with some rice kernels on it stir the beef and break it up with a spoon.

8. Using a plate, scoop a portion of rice, top with the beef and a bit of the juices or you may top with green onions and sesame seeds as you desire.

9. Serve immediately and enjoy!!!

Pork Tenderloin Teriyaki

Preparation time: 15 minutes

Cooking time: 35 minutes

Total time: 50 minutes

Servings: 5

Ingredients:

- 2 ¹/² green onions chopped
- 2 tbsp. oil
- 2 ¹/² cups of teriyaki sauce
- toasted sesame seeds
- 2 pork tenderloins (cut in half length)
- salt and pepper to taste

Cooking Instructions:

1. Take a bowl and season the pork with salt and pepper. Switch on your Instant Pot and set to sauté mode, and put the oil in the bottom.

2. Observe when the pan is hot then put the meat making sure it browns both sides of them.

3. When you are satisfied frying the meat, put them down in the cooker and pour the teriyaki sauce over the top.

4. Close and lock the lid in place and ensure that the valve is in sealing position. Press the manual function to cook on high pressure for about 20 minutes.

5. When the time is up, use a natural pressure release for about 12 minutes. Carefully open the lid once the pressure has been released. Shred the meat.

6. Scoop jasmine rice, steamed broccoli and garnish with toasted sesame seeds and chopped green onions.

7. Serve and enjoy.

Beef Pot Roast

Preparation time: 15 minutes

Cooking time: 1 hour 45 minutes

Total time: 2 hours

Servings: 7

Ingredients:

- 2 ¹/₂ tbsp. corn starch
- 1 big bag carrots, peeled and chopped
- 4 ¹/₂ (1 oz) packets of McCormick Brown Gravy Mix
- 1 cup brewed coffee
- 10 oz red wine (cabernet)
- ½ cup of reduced sodium soy sauce
- 3 tbsp. Worcestershire sauce
- 2 tsp. freshly cracked black pepper
- 3 lb. bottom round roast
- 6 big cloves garlic, diced
- 1 big sweet yellow onion, chopped
- 2 cups of sliced Portobello mushrooms
- 2 tbsp. oil

Cooking Instructions:

1. Whisk together McCormick Brown Gravy Mix and cornstarch in a big container. To avoid lumps, whisk in coffee gently.

2. Whisk in wine, soy sauce, Worcestershire sauce, garlic and black pepper. Keep them in one corner.

3. Set Instant Pot to sauté mode. Put oil to pot and quickly sear meat on all sides. Switch off sauté mode.

4. Top meat with carrots, onion and mushrooms, gravy mix on top and keep lid on Instant pot with steam valve closed.

5. Close and lock the lid in place and ensure that the valve is in sealing position. Press the manual settings to cook on high pressure for about 45 minutes.

6. When the time is up, use a natural pressure release for about 15 minutes.

7. Carefully remove roast from Instant Pot, shred with forks, put gravy and vegetables to mix well.

8. Scoop your dish into a plate, top with gravy and vegetables over mashed potatoes.

9. Serve and enjoy!!!

Smothered Pork Chops

Preparation time: 15 minutes

Cooking time: 27 minutes

Total time: 42 minutes

Servings: 5

Ingredients:

- 1 tbsp. butter
- 1 tbsp. paprika
- 1 ¹/₂ tsp. onion powder
- ½ tsp. xanthan gum
- 1 tsp. black pepper
- 1 tsp. salt
- ¼ tsp. cayenne pepper
- 2 tbsp. coconut oil
- ½ medium onion, sliced
- 5 oz. sliced baby bella mushrooms
- ½ cup of heavy cream
- 1 tbsp chopped fresh parsley
- 4 (6 oz) boneless pork loin chops
- 1¹/² tsp. garlic powder

Cooking Instructions:

1. Combine and mix these ingredients together in a small container - paprika, garlic powder, onion powder, black pepper, salt, and cayenne pepper

2. Wash the pork chops and pat dry. Spray both sides of the pork chops with 1 ¹/² tbsp of the spice mixture, rubbing the seasoning into the meat. Do not use all the spices.

3. Set the Instant Pot on the Sauté mode put the coconut oil in the bowl of the pot.

4. Sauté the pork chops to brown for about 3 minutes per side and remove the pork chops from the Instant Pot when you are satisfied with the sauté.

5. Put the sliced onions and mushrooms into the Instant Pot. Add the browned pork chops.

6. Close and lock the lid in place and ensure that the valve is in sealing position. Press the manual key to cook on high pressure for about 30 minutes.

7. When the time is up, use a natural pressure release for about 12 minutes. Open the pot lid and place just the pork chops on a serving plate.

8. Reset the Sauté mode again and whisk the remaining spice mixture, butter, and heavy cream into the hot liquid.

9. Pour half tsp of xanthan gum into the liquid and whisk in immediately. Let the gravy simmer for 5 minutes until the butter is melted and the sauce starts to thicken.

10. Switch off the Instant Pot. Start with ¼ tsp of xanthan gum and put additional until the gravy thickens to your desired taste.

11. Serve and enjoy!!!

Steamed Alaskan Crab Legs

Preparation time: 6 minutes

Cooking time: 5 minutes

Total time: 11 minutes

Servings: 5

Ingredients:

- 1 cup of water
- 3 lbs. frozen crab legs
- Melted butter for serving
- ½ tbsp. salt

Cooking Instructions:

1. Put steamer basket into Instant Pot with 1 cup of water and ½ tbsp of salt.

2. Put half of the Alaskan King Crab Legs with 1 tbsp of salt.

3. Close and lock the lid in place and ensure that the valve is in sealing position.

4. Press the manual key to cook on high pressure for about 5 minutes.

5. When the time is up, use a natural pressure release for about 7 minutes.

6. Carefully open the lid of your Instant Pot when the pin has dropped (this can take few minutes).

7. Remove crab legs and top with melted butter.

8. Serve and enjoy!!!

10-Minute Instant Pot Salmon

Preparation time: 6 minutes

Cooking time: 5 minutes

Total time: 11 minutes

Servings: 5

Ingredients:

- 5 fillet salmon
- 2 medium lemon
- 1 tbsp. butter, unsalted
- ¼ tsp. salt
- ¼ tsp. black pepper, ground
- ¾ cup of water
- 1 bunch of dill weed, fresh

Optional Toppings:

- 1 cup of brown rice, raw
- 4 cup of green beans

Cooking Instructions:

1. Put ¼ cup fresh lemon juice, ¾ cup of water in the bottom of the Instant Pot.

2. Put the metal steamer insert and put the salmon fillets, frozen, on top of the steamer insert.

3. Spray fresh dill on top of the salmon, and then keep one slice of fresh lemon on top of each one.

4. Close and lock the lid in place and ensure that the valve is in sealing position

5. Press the manual button to cook on high pressure for about 5 minutes.

6. When the time is up, use a natural pressure release for about 8 minutes.

7. Carefully open the lid and give everything a good stir.

8. Serve immediately and enjoy!!!

Shrimp Scampi

Preparation time: 6 minutes

Cooking time: 10 minutes

Total time: 16 minutes

Servings: 4

Ingredients:

- 1 tbsp. fresh squeezed lemon juice
- 2 tbsp. extra virgin olive oil
- 2 tbsp. pastured butter
- 1 tbsp. minced organic garlic
- ½ cup of white wine
- 2 lbs. shrimp
- 1 lb. gluten free pasta or 3 cups cooked rice
- Sea salt and pepper, to taste
- Parsley, optional garnish
- ½ cup of homemade chicken stock

Cooking Instructions

1. Put the oil and butter in your Instant Pot, closing the lid and set the pot to Sauté mode.

2. Heat the butter for sometimes and put the garlic and cook just until fragrant.

3. Put the white wine and chicken stock to deglaze the Instant Pot. Stir up any browned bits.

4. Close and lock the lid in place and ensure that the valve is in sealing position

5. Press the manual setting to cook on high pressure for about 5 minutes.

6. When the time is up, use a natural pressure release for about 5 minutes.

7. Carefully open the lid and sprinkle the cooked pasta or rice. Add the lemon juice, salt and pepper to taste.

8. Serve immediately and enjoy!!!

Lemon Pepper Salmon

Preparation time: 6 minutes

Cooking time: 10 minutes

Total time: 16 minutes

Servings: 5

Ingredients

- 1 carrot chopped
- ¾ cup of water
- 1 lb. salmon filet skin on
- 1 zucchini chopped
- 3 tsp. ghee
- ¼ tsp. salt or to taste
- ½ tsp. pepper or to taste
- ½ lemon thinly sliced
- 1 red bell pepper chopped
- A few sprigs of parsley dill, tarragon or a combo

Cooking Instructions:

1. Add water and herbs in the Instant Pot and then put in the steamer rack making sure the handles are properly extended.

2. Put salmon, skin down on rack and mix salmon with ghee/fat, season with salt and pepper, and cover with lemon slices.

3. Close and lock the lid in place and ensure that the valve is in sealing position

4. Press the manual key to cook on high pressure for about 10 minutes.

5. When the time is up, use a natural pressure release for about 7 minutes.

6. Garnish your veggies while salmon is still being cooked.

7. Carefully open the lid, and using hot pads, carefully remove rack with salmon and set on a plate.

8. Remove herbs and discard. Put veggies and put the lid back on. Press "Sauté" and let the veggies cook for just 3 minutes.

9. Put the remaining teaspoon of fat to the pot and pour small amount of the sauce over them if desired.

10. Serve and enjoy!!!

Coconut Fish Curry
Preparation time: 6 minutes

Cooking time: 10 minutes

Total time: 16 minutes

Servings: 5

Ingredients:

- ½ tsp. ground Turmeric
- 2 lb (680g) Fish steaks or fillets, rinsed and cut into pieces
- 1 Tomato, chopped
- 2 ½ Green Chiles, sliced into strips
- 2 Medium onions, sliced into strips
- ½ tsp. Ground Fenugreek (Methi)
- 2 Garlic cloves, squeezed
- ½ tsp. ground Turmeric
- 8 Curry leaves or Bay Laurel Leaves
- 1 tbsp. ground Coriander
- ½ tsp. ground Turmeric
- 2 tsp. ground Cumin
- 1 tsp. Chili powder, or 1 tsp. of Hot Pepper Flakes

Cooking Instructions:

1. Heat the cooker on a low heat pressure without the lid, put a little oil into the Instant Pot and then put the curry leaves and lightly fry for about a minute.

2. Put onion, garlic, and ginger and sauté until the onion is soft.

3. Put all of the ground spices: coriander, cumin, turmeric, chili powder and fenugreek. Sauté them together with the onions until they have released their aroma (about 2 minutes).

4. Deglaze with the coconut milk making sure to unstick anything from the bottom of the cooker and incorporate it into the sauce.

5. Put the Green Chiles, tomatoes and fish pieces. Stir to coat the fish well with the mixture.

6. Close and lock the lid in place and ensure that the valve is in sealing position.

7. Press the manual function to cook on low pressure for about 7 minutes.

8. When the time is up, use a natural pressure release for about 10 minutes.

9. Carefully open the lid and add salt to taste. Spritz with lemon juice just before serving.

10. Serve and enjoy!!!

Sweet & Spicy Pineapple

Preparation time: 6 minutes

Cooking time: 7 minutes

Total time: 13 minutes

Servings: 5

Ingredients:

- 1 tbsp. Sambal Oelek Ground Chili Paste
- 2 tbsp. Soy Sauce
- 1 big Red Bell Pepper cleaned and sliced
- 10 oz. Calrose Rice or Quinoa
- 1.5 cups of Unsweetened Pineapple Chunks drained
- 3/4 cup of Unsweetened Pineapple Juice
- ¼ cup of Dry White Wine
- 2 tbsp. Thai Sweet Chili Sauce
- 1 lb. big Shrimp, tails on frozen
- 4 Scallions chopped, White and Greens separated

Cooking Instructions:

1. Get juice from pineapple and keep pineapple chunks aside. Measure out ¾ cup of pineapple Juice.

2. Add the red bell peppers, pineapple juice, wine, chili sauce, soy sauce, sambal Oelek, and rice and chopped scallions (the white part) to Instant Pot.

3. Place the frozen shrimp on top. Close and lock the lid in place and ensure that the valve is in sealing position.

4. Press the manual setting to cook on high pressure for about 3 minutes. When the time is up, use a natural pressure release for about 8 minutes.

5. Carefully open the lid once the pressure has been released. Put your pineapple Chunks and Scallion Greens and mix through.

6. Serve immediately and enjoy!!!

Fish Tacos

Preparation time: 6 minutes

Cooking time: 7 minutes

Total time: 13 minutes

Servings: 5

Ingredients:

- 2 sprigs of fresh cilantro.
- 2 tilapia fillets
- Salt to taste
- 2 tbsp. of smoked paprika
- juice of one lime
- 1 tsp. of canola oil

Cooking Instruction

1. Use a large parchment paper and put tilapia in the middle.

2. Using canola oil paint the tilapia, spray with salt and paprika, squeeze lime juice on the tilapia and sprinkle with some cilantro.

3. Bend or fold your old parchment paper into a packet and keep no space for air ventilation.

4. Put 1 1/2 cups of water in the bottom of your Instant Pot, along with the trivet.

5. Close and lock the lid in place and ensure that the valve is in sealing position.

6. Press the manual function to cook on high pressure for about 7 minutes.

7. When the time is up, use a natural pressure release for about 5 minutes.

8. Cut the fish according to how you want to place it on a taco. Build your taco to your choice.

9. Serve immediately and enjoy!!!

4 Minute Salmon, Broccoli & Potatoes

Preparation time: 2 minutes

Cooking time: 6 minutes

Total time: 8 minutes

Servings: 3

Ingredients:

- 70 g Broccoli
- 230 g New Potatoes
- $1^{1/2}$ tsp. Butter
- Salt & Pepper
- Fresh Herbs optional
- 7 g Salmon Fillet

Cooking Instructions:

1. Shred broccoli into florets and put to one side.

2. Put 150ml of water into the bottom of your Instant Pot.

3. Put potatoes into Instant Pot, use salt, pepper and fresh herbs to season. Also Season your salmon and broccoli with salt and pepper.

4. Put your potatoes into the steaming rack and smother them with the butter so that the butter will melt as you cook them.

5. Close and lock the lid in place and ensure that the valve is in sealing position. Press the manual key to cook on high pressure for about 4 minutes.

6. When the time is up, use a natural pressure release for about 5 minutes.

7. Put your broccoli florets and salmon onto the rack and cook in the same way for about 4 minutes.

8. Serve and enjoy!!!

Salmon with Chili-Lime Sauce

Preparation time: 7 minutes

Cooking time: 8 minutes

Total time: 15 minutes

Calories: 380 kcal

Servings: 3

Ingredients:

For steaming salmon:

- 1 tbsp olive oil
- 2 cloves garlic minced
- 2 salmon fillets 5 oz each
- 1 cup of water
- ½ tsp. paprika
- salt to taste
- Black pepper to taste (freshly ground)

For chili-lime sauce:

- 1 ½ lime juiced
- 1 1/2 tbsp. honey
- 1 tbsp. hot water
- 1 tbsp. chopped fresh parsley
- ½ tsp. cumin
- 1 jalapeno seeds removed and diced

Cooking Instructions:

1. Gather all the sauce ingredients and mix in a bowl and keep aside when done.

2. Put water to the pressure cooker and put salmon fillets on top of a steam rack inside the Instant Pot.

3. Put salt and pepper to your taste on top of the salmon fillets and season.

4. Close and lock the lid in place and ensure that the valve is in sealing position.

5. Press the manual button to cook on high pressure for about 8 minutes.

6. When the time is up, use a natural pressure release for about 7 minutes.

7. Carefully open the lid once the pressure has been released and transfer the salmon to a serving plate.

8. Garnish with chili-lime sauce.

9. Serve and enjoy!!!

Savory Shrimp with Tomatoes & Feta

Preparation time: 8 minutes

Cooking time: 15 minutes

Total time: 23 minutes

Calories: 280 kcal

Servings: 6

Ingredients:

Cook Together:

- 1 tsp. oregano
- 1 tbsp. garlic
- 1.5 cups of chopped onion
- 1 15 oz can tomatoes
- 1 tsp. salt
- ½ tsp. red pepper flakes adjust to taste
- 1 lb. frozen shrimp 21-25 count, shelled
- 2 tbsp. Butter

Add after cooking:

- ¼ cup of sliccd black olives
- 1 cup of crumbled feta cheese
- 1/3 cup of parsley

Cooking Instructions:

1. Set your Instant Pot to Sauté and put the butter when it is hot.

2. Allow it to melt a little and then put garlic and red pepper flakes, onions, tomatoes, oregano and salt and pour the frozen shrimp.

3. Close and lock the lid in place and ensure that the valve is in sealing position. Press the manual function to cook on low pressure for about 2 minutes.

4. When the time is up, use a natural pressure release for about 5 minutes. Mix in the shrimp with all the tomato broth. Allow it to cool for a while. Pour the feta cheese, olives, and parsley on top.

5. Serve and enjoy!!!

Crustless Crab Quiche

Preparation time: 15 minutes

Cooking time: 53 minutes

Total time: 1 hour 8 minutes

Calories: 380 kcal

Servings: 6

Ingredients:

- 1 tsp. sweet smoked paprika
- 5 eggs
- 1 cup half and half
- 10 oz. real crab meat, or a mix of crab and chopped raw shrimp
- 1 tsp. salt
- 1 tsp. pepper
- 1 tsp. Herbes de Provence
- 1 cup of shredded cheese
- 1 cup of chopped green onions green and white parts

Cooking Instructions:

1. Using a large bowl, mix together eggs and half-and-half with a whisk.

2. Put salt, pepper, sweet smoked paprika, Herbes de Provence, and shredded cheese, chopped green onions and stir with a fork to mix completely.

3. Put the real crab meat OR some combination of crab meat and chopped raw shrimp.

4. Spread out a sheet of aluminum foil that is cut bigger than the pan you want to use. Place the spring form pan on this sheet and crimp the sheet about the bottom.

5. Put the egg mixture into your spring form pan. Loosely close with foil or a silicone lid.

6. Put 2 cups of water into the inner pot of your Instant Pot and put a steamer rack in the pot. Put the covered spring form pan on the trivet.

7. Close and lock the lid in place and ensure that the valve is in sealing position. Press the manual key to cook on high pressure for about 50 minutes.

8. When the time is up, use a natural pressure release for about 10 minutes. Carefully remove the hot silicone pan.

9. With your knife, loosen the edges of the quiche from the pan. Remove the outer ring. Your dish is ready.

10. Serve and enjoy!!!

VEGAN & VEGETARIAN
Vegan Butter Chicken with Soy Curls & Chickpeas
Preparation time: 11 minutes

Cooking time: 33 minutes

Total time: 44 minutes

Calories: 380 kcal

Servings: 5

Ingredients:

- ½ tsp. cayenne
- 4 big ripe tomatoes
- 3 cloves of garlic
- ½ inch cube of ginger
- 1 cup of water
- 1 tsp. graham masala
- ½ tsp. paprika or Kashmiri chili powder
- ¾ tsp. salt
- 1 cup of soy curls (dry, not rehydrated)
- 1 cup of cooked chickpeas
- Cashew cream made with ¼ cup of soaked cashews blended with ½ cup of water
- ½ tsp. or more graham masala
- ½ tsp. or more sugar or sweetener
- ½ moderately hot green chili finely chopped, or use 2 tbsp finely chopped green bell pepper
- ½ tsp. minced or finely chopped ginger
- ¼ cup of cilantro for garnish
- 1 hot or mild green chili
- 1 tsp. kasoori methi - dried fenugreek leaves or add a ¼ tsp ground mustard

Cooking Instructions:

1. Mix together tomatoes, garlic, ginger, chili and blend with water until smooth.

2. Put pureed tomato mixture to the Instant Pot or pressure cooker. Put soy curls, chickpeas, spices and salt.

3. Close and lock the lid in place and ensure that the valve is in sealing position. Press the manual key to cook on high pressure for about 10 minutes.

4. When the time is up, use a natural pressure release for about 10 minutes. Carefully open the lid once the pressure has been released.

5. Set the Instant Pot on sauté and put the cashew cream, graham masala, sweetener and fenugreek leaves and mix in. Bring to a boil, taste and adjust salt, heat, sweet.

6. You may put more cayenne and salt if needed. Fold in the chopped green chili, ginger and cilantro and press cancel on the Instant Pot.

7. You may also put some vegan butter or oil for additional buttery flavor.

8. Serve immediately and enjoy!!!

Maple Bourbon Sweet Potato Chili

Preparation time: 10 minutes

Cooking time: 23 minutes

Total time: 33 minutes

Calories: 220 kcal

Servings: 5

Ingredients:

- 4 cloves garlic, minced
- 1 tbsp. cooking oil
- 1 small yellow onion, thinly sliced
- 2 (14) oz cans kidney beans, drained and rinsed
- A few fresh springs of cilantro
- 4 ½ cups of sweet potatoes, peeled and cut into 1/2" pieces
- 2 cups vegetable broth
- 1 ½ tbsp. chili powder
- ½ tsp. paprika
- 1/3 tsp. cayenne pepper
- 1 (15) oz can minced tomatoes
- ¼ cup of bourbon
- 2 tbsp. maple syrup
- salt and pepper, to taste
- 2 green onions, minced
- 3 small corn tortillas, toasted and sliced (optional)
- 2 tsp. cumin

Cooking Instructions:

1. Set your Instant Pot to sauté, put oil, and let it heat up for 40 seconds.

2. Put onions and heat up for about 5 minutes, stir it periodically, until onions are fragrant. Put garlic and heat for another 40 seconds.

3. Put shredded sweet potatoes, chili powder, cumin, paprika, and cayenne pepper, stir until vegetables are well coated.

4. Put vegetable broth, beans, tomatoes, maple syrup, and bourbon. Close and lock the lid in place and ensure that the valve is in sealing position.

5. Press the manual setting to cook on high pressure for about 15 minutes. When the time is up, use a natural pressure release for about 12 minutes.

6. Carefully open the lid and check to make sure the sweet potatoes are tender.

7. If you are making use of tortillas, lightly oil a cast iron skillet and pan sauté the tortillas on each side for 3 minutes.

8. Carefully remove from heat and let cool before shredding into thin strips.

9. You may add these optional toppings: cilantro, green onions, and toasted tortillas.

10. Serve and enjoy!!!

Easy Vegan Mashed Potatoes

Preparation time: 8 minutes

Cooking time: 23 minutes

Total time: 31 minutes

Calories: 90 kcal

Servings: 5

Ingredients:

- 5 cloves of garlic
- 6 potatoes cubed into large pieces Yukon gold
- ½ tsp. salt
- 1 ½ tbsp. extra virgin olive oil or vegan butter
- dash of parsley or thyme
- pinch of nutmeg
- 1 cup of full fat coconut milk
- fresh chives for garnish
- a good dash of black pepper

Cooking Instructions:

1. Mix and cook the cubed potatoes, garlic cloves, ¼ tsp. salt with 1.5 cups of water.

2. Close and lock the lid in place and ensure that the valve is in sealing position

3. Press the manual key to cook on high pressure for about 5 minutes. When the time is up, use a natural pressure release for about 5 minutes.

4. You may also boil them in a saucepan. Add the potatoes into a large pot, adding enough water to cover them.

5. Boil for about 15 minutes, until they are soft. Remove them to a colander to drain very well.

6. Turn into a bowl, let sit for a few minutes to dry out. Mash lightly and let sit for a minute for the steam to escape.

7. Mash the cooked garlic. Put salt and the rest of the ingredients and half cup of coconut milk.

8. Mix and whip lightly, just enough to add air and still have some texture. Allow to rest for a minute for the milks to incorporate and absorb.

9. Put $1/3$ tsp. or more salt as needed. Put more coconut milk to be creamier if needed and mix thoroughly.

10. Put 2 tbsp. nutritional yeast for cheesy potatoes. Garnish with chives.

11. Serve and enjoy!!!

Walnut Lentil Tacos

Preparation time: 5 minutes

Cooking time: 10 minutes

Total time: 15 minutes

Yield: 11-12 tacos

Ingredients:

- ½ tsp. garlic powder
- 1 white onion, diced
- 1 ½ tbsp. olive oil
- 1 cup of dried brown lentils
- 2 garlic clove, minced
- 1 tbsp. chili powder
- ¼ tsp. onion powder
- 1/3 tsp. red pepper flakes
- 1 ½ tsp. ground cumin
- ½ tsp. kosher salt
- 1/3 tsp. freshly ground pepper
- 2 ½ cups of vegetable broth
- 1/2 tsp. paprika
- 1 14 oz can fire-roasted diced tomatoes
- ¾ cup of chopped walnuts
- 1/3 tsp. oregano

Taco toppings of choice: shredded lettuce, tomato, jalapenos, flour or corn tortillas

Cooking Instructions:

1. Switch the Instant Pot on and press the Sauté button.

2. Put the olive oil, onion and garlic clove and sauté until onion cooked through and stir occasionally for about 4 minutes.

3. Put the spices and stir together. Press cancel and put the vegetable broth, tomatoes, walnuts and lentils and stir to mix well.

4. Close and lock the lid in place and ensure that the valve is in sealing position.

5. Press the manual button to cook on high pressure for about 10 minutes.

6. When the time is up, use a natural pressure release for about 4 minutes.

7. Carefully open the lid and stir lentils, seasoning to taste if needed.

8. You may add toppings of your choice.

9. Serve immediately and enjoy!!!

Cilantro Lime Quinoa

Preparation time: 6 minutes

Cooking time: 10 minutes

Total time: 16 minutes

Calories: 97 kcal

Servings: 5

Ingredients:

- 2 tbsp. lime juice
- 1 cup of quinoa rinsed and drained (any color)
- salt to taste
- zest of one lime
- ½ cup of chopped cilantro
- 1 ¼ cups of vegetable broth

Cooking Instructions:

1. Put the quinoa and 1 ¼ cup vegetable broth to the Instant Pot.

2. Close and lock the lid in place and ensure that the valve is in sealing position.

3. Press the manual key to cook on high pressure for about 5 minutes.

4. When the time is up, use a natural pressure release for about 7 minutes.

5. Carefully open the lid and pour the lime juice, lime zest, and cilantro. Taste and add salt to taste.

6. Serve and enjoy!!!

Vegan Lentil Chili

Preparation time: 10 minutes

Cooking time: 22 minutes

Total time: 32 minutes

Servings: 5

Ingredients:

- 1 tsp. dried oregano
- 1 onion, chopped
- 4 cloves minced garlic
- 2 carrots, chopped
- 2 jalapeños, chopped
- 1 ½ tbsp. chili powder
- ½ tsp. ground coriander
- ½ tsp. salt
- ½ cup of chopped fresh cilantro
- 1 14 oz can crushed tomatoes
- 1 30 oz can fire roasted diced tomatoes
- 1 tbsp. olive oil
- 2 cups of brown or green lentils.
- 4 ½ cups of vegetable broth
- 1 tsp. fresh lime juice
- 1 tbsp, cumin

Cooking Instructions:

1. Put olive oil in the Instant Pot, hit the sauté button on the Instant Pot and heat the oil for sometimes.

2. Put the onion, garlic, carrots and jalapeños and heat until soft, about 4 minutes. Put the spices and remaining ingredients except for lime juice and cilantro.

3. Close and lock the lid in place and ensure that the valve is in sealing position. Press the manual function to cook on high pressure for about 15 minutes.

4. When the time is up, use a natural pressure release for about 10 minutes. Carefully open the lid once the pressure has been released. Pour lime juice and cilantro.

5. Serve immediately and enjoy!

Mushroom Risotto

Preparation time: 12 minutes

Cooking time: 20 minutes

Total time: 32 minutes

Calories: 370 kcal

Servings: 5

Ingredients:

- 1 ½ tbsp. olive oil
- 2 ½ tbsp. vegan butter, divided
- 1 medium onion, diced
- 4 cloves garlic, minced
- 10 oz. cremini mushrooms dry brushed & minced
- ¾ tsp. dried thyme
- 1 ½ cups of Arborio rice
- ½ cup of dry white wine
- 4 cups of vegetable broth, low sodium
- 1 ¼ tsp. sea salt, more to taste
- Fresh ground pepper to taste
- 1 cup of frozen peas, thawed
- 4 tbsp. Vegan Parmesan Cheese (optional)

Cooking Instructions:

1. Switch on the Sauté mode of your Instant Pot and put the oil and butter. Heat the oil; put the onions and sauté about 3 minutes.

2. Put the garlic and thyme and sauté for a minute. You can now put the mushrooms and sauté for about 4 minutes until soft.

3. Put the rice and stir to coat well. Pour the wine and cook until the liquid mostly cooks down. About 2 minutes. Put the broth, salt, and pepper.

4. Close and lock the lid in place and ensure that the valve is in sealing position. Press the manual setting to cook on high pressure for about 6 minutes.

5. When the time is up, use a natural pressure release for about 6 minutes. Note the risotto will look soupy when you first remove the lid.

6. Just stir for sometimes and it will thicken up. Put the peas, butter, and vegan parmesan. If you need some seasoning, you may add it.

7. Top with fresh-cut parsley, crushed red pepper flakes, and fresh cracked pepper.

8. Serve and enjoy!!!

Vegan Potato Curry

Preparation time: 12 minutes

Cooking time: 45 minutes

Total time: 57 minutes

Calories: 270 kcal

Servings: 5

Ingredients:

- 1 420ml can coconut milk, full fat or light
- 1 medium yellow onion, chopped
- 4 large cloves of garlic, chopped finely
- 950g and about 5 heaping cups baby potatoes
- 2 tbsp. curry powder or curry paste
- 500mls and around 2 cups water
- 3 tbsp. arrowroot powder.
- 1 tbsp. sugar
- Salt and pepper to taste
- 1 tsp. chili pepper flakes or a small fresh chili chopped
- 400g and 2 heaping cups fresh green beans, chopped into small sizes

Cooking Instructions:

1. Turn your Instant Pot to sauté mode.

2. When it is hot, put a few drops of water and cook the onions until soft.

3. Add the garlic and cook for one minute. Press the keep warm/cancel button.

4. Add everything else to the Instant Pot except the green beans and arrowroot.

5. Close and lock the lid in place and ensure that the valve is in sealing position.

6. Press the manual key to cook on high pressure for about 20 minutes.

7. When the time is up, use a natural pressure release for about 16 minutes.

8. Add the arrowroot into a small bowl and pour a few tbsp of water to make it thick.

9. Pour it into the Instant Pot stirring continuously. Add salt and pepper to taste then add the green beans.

10. Cook for about 5 minutes until they are soft and the gravy has thickened.

11. Serve immediately and enjoy!!!

Carrot Ginger Soup

Preparation time: 15 minutes

Cooking time: 17 minutes

Total time: 32 minutes

Calories: 270 kcal

Servings: 5

Ingredients:

- 2 tbsp. grape seed oil or preferred oil
- 1 medium onion, diced
- 4 cloves garlic , minced
- 1.5 tbsp. fresh ginger, grated
- 1 tsp. dried thyme
- ½ tsp. ground coriander
- ½ tsp. crushed red pepper
- 2 bay leaves
- 2 lb. carrots (about 6 large), rough chopped
- 4 cups of vegetable broth, low sodium
- 1 tsp. sea salt, more to taste
- Fresh cracked pepper to taste (optional)
- 1 cup of canned coconut milk , full-fat
- 2 tbsp. lime juice (sub lemon)

Cooking Instructions:

1. Switch on the sauté mode of your Instant Pot and add the oil.

2. When the oil has heated, add the onions and sauté for about 3 minutes.

3. Put the garlic and ginger, sauté for 2 minutes. Put thyme, coriander and crushed red pepper. Sauté for 50 seconds.

4. Cancel the sauté function and put the broth, carrots, bay leaves, salt, and cracked pepper.

5. Close and lock the lid in place and ensure that the valve is in sealing position. Press the manual button to cook on high pressure for about 6 minutes.

6. When the time is up, use a natural pressure release for about 3 minutes. Set the steam release handle to the venting position.

7. Carefully open the lid and remove the bay leaves and put the coconut milk and lime juice.

8. Using a regular blender, blend until smooth. Taste for seasoning and put more if you desire

9. If for any reason, the soup is too thick for your taste, you can add a small amount of vegetable broth to thin it out.

10. Serve immediately and enjoy!!!

Prosciutto-wrapped Asparagus Canes
Preparation time: 5 minutes

Cooking time: 7 minutes

Total time: 12 minutes

Servings: 5

Ingredients:

- 1 lb. (480g) thick Asparagus
- 8 oz. (235g) thinly sliced Prosciutto

Cooking Instructions:

1. Add small amount of water (1 to 2 cups) into your Instant Pot and keep aside.

2. Take the asparagus spears and wrap in prosciutto. Place any extra un-wrapped spears in a single layer on the bottom of the steamer basket to prevent the prosciutto from sticking.

3. Put the prosciutto-wrapped asparagus on top in a single layer also. Keep the basket inside the Instant pot.

4. Close and lock the lid in place and ensure that the valve is in sealing position. Press the manual key to cook on high pressure for about 3 minutes.

5. When the time is up, use a natural pressure release for about 5 minutes. Carefully open the lid once the pressure has been released.

6. Get the steamer basket out immediately and place the asparagus on a serving platter so they may not be gradually cooked by remaining heat.

7. Serve immediately and enjoy!!!

Black Bean Dip
Preparation time: 20 minutes

Cooking time: 33 minutes

Total time: 53 minutes

Servings: 25

Ingredients:

- 1 medium onion, diced
- 3 cloves of garlic, peeled + minced
- 2 medium jalapeños (approx. 1/3 cup chopped)
- 1 ½ cup of vegetable broth
- 1 ½ tbsp. avocado oil
- juice of 1 lime
- Chopped tomatoes, sliced jalapeños, diced bell pepper, chopped red onion, cilantro, sour cream for toppings
- 2 tsp. ground cumin
- 1 tsp. smoked paprika
- ¾ tsp. sea salt
- 1 ½ cup of dried black beans
- ½ tsp. chili powder
- ½ tsp. ground coriander
- 1 (15 oz) can diced or crushed tomatoes.

Cooking Instructions:

1. Wash your black beans and put them in your Instant Pot.

2. Dice and chop your veggies and mince your garlic. Put veggies, garlic, tomatoes, broth, oil, lime juice, and spices to the pot and mix.

3. Close and lock the lid in place and ensure that the valve is in sealing position.

4. Press the manual button to cook on high pressure for about 25 minutes.

5. When the time is up, use a natural pressure release for about 10 minutes.

6. With a blender or food processor, blend the tip all together and taste it when it is cool.

7. You can add more spice either from hot sauce, spicy salsa, red pepper flakes, or cayenne to the mix.

8. Add any extra spices and salt to suit your tastes.

9. Serve and enjoy!!!

Cocktail Meatballs

Preparation time: 5 minutes

Cooking time: 7 minutes

Total time: 12 minutes

Serves: 65 pieces

Ingredients:

- 1 tbsp. minced garlic
- 2 lb. cooked Perfect Homestyle Meatballs
- ¼ cup of honey
- ½ cup of ketchup
- 2 tbsp. soy sauce
- ⅓ cup of brown sugar
- Garnish with sliced green onions (optional)

Cooking Instructions:

1. Mix brown sugar, honey, ketchup, soy sauce, and garlic in pressure cooker.

2. Set to sauté mode and stir to mix properly.

3. When the mixture comes to a boil, put the frozen fully cooked meatballs.

4. Close and lock the lid in place and ensure that the valve is in sealing position.

5. Press the manual function to cook on high pressure for about 5 minutes.

6. When the time is up, use a natural pressure release for about 3 minutes.

7. Serve hot and enjoy!!!

Buffalo Ranch Chicken Dip

Preparation time: 5 minutes

Cooking time: 20 minutes

Total time: 25 minutes

Calories: 506 kcal

Servings: 6

Ingredients:

- 1 ½ lb. chicken breast
- 1 packet ranch dip
- 1 ½ cup of Hot Sauce
- 1 stick butter
- 15 oz cheddar cheese
- 8 oz cream cheese

Cooking Instructions:

1. Put chicken, cream cheese, butter, hot sauce, and a packet of ranch dip in your Instant Pot.
2. Close and lock the lid in place and ensure that the valve is in sealing position.
3. Press the manual key to cook on high pressure for about 15 minutes.
4. When the time is up, use a natural pressure release for about 5 minutes.
5. Carefully open the lid once the pressure has been released.
6. Shred your chicken with fork or use your mixer to break it up and pour cheddar cheese.
7. Have some chips available.
8. Serve and enjoy!!!

Cranberry Pecan Brie
Preparation time: 15 minutes

Cooking time: 30 minutes

Total time: 45 minutes

Servings: 4

Ingredients:

- 1 (8-oz) round of Brie
- ¼ cup of cranberry jalapeno preserves
- 3 tbsp. candied pecans
- 1 tsp. minced fresh thyme

Cooking Instructions:

1. Slice through the rind on top of the Brie in a grid pattern.

2. Put the Brie in a baking dish in a way it will fit in your instant pot and then cover baking dish tightly with foil.

3. Prepare a foil sling for lifting the baking dish out of the Instant Pot by taking an 18" strip of foil and folding it twice.

4. Put 1 cup of water into the Instant Pot and place the rack in the bottom.

5. Keep the baking dish on center of the foil strip and lower it into the instant pot on to the rack. Fold the foil strips down so they may not disturb you when closing the lid.

6. Close and lock the lid in place and ensure that the valve is in sealing position. Press the manual setting to cook on high pressure for about 20 minutes.

7. When the time is up, use a natural pressure release for about 10 minutes. You can now inspect to make sure cheese is melted and piping hot.

8. Scoop to a serving plate and top with preserves, pecans and thyme.

9. Serve immediately and enjoy!!!

Beer-Braised Pulled Ham
Preparation time: 15 minutes

Cooking time: 30 minutes

Total time: 45 minutes

Servings: 14

Ingredients:

- ½ tsp. coarsely ground pepper
- 2 bottles (12 oz each) beer or nonalcoholic beer
- 3/4 cup of German or Dijon mustard, divided
- 1 fully cooked bone-in ham (4 lb)
- 16 pretzel hamburger buns, split
- Dill pickle slices (optional)
- 4 fresh rosemary sprigs

Cooking Instructions:

1. Whisk together beer, ½ cup of mustard and pepper into your Instant Pot.

2. Put ham and rosemary. Close and lock the lid in place and ensure that the valve is in sealing position

3. Press the manual key to cook on high pressure for about 20 minutes. When the time is up, use a natural pressure release for about 15 minutes.

4. Carefully remove ham and allow it to cool. Discard rosemary sprigs. Skim fat from liquid remaining in Instant Pot.

5. Select sauté mode and set on high pressure. Boil your liquid for about 7 minutes.

6. Touch the ham. When it is cool enough to handle, cut meat with two forks.

7. Replace ham to Instant Pot; heat through.

8. Serve and enjoy!!!

Mini Teriyaki Turkey Sandwiches

Preparation time: 15 minutes

Cooking time: 30 minutes

Total time: 45 minutes

Servings: 24

Ingredients:

- 2 tbsp. cornstarch
- 2/3 cup of packed brown sugar
- 2/3 cup of less-sodium soy sauce
- 1/3 cup of cider vinegar
- 4 garlic cloves, minced
- 1 tbsp. minced fresh gingerroot
- 1 ½ tsp. pepper
- 2 tbsp. butter, melted
- 2 tbsp. cold water
- 20 Hawaiian sweet rolls
- 2 boneless skinless turkey breast halves (2 ½ lbs each)

Cooking Instructions:

1. Put turkey into your Instant Pot. Using a small bowl, mix the ingredients with the turkey.

2. Close and lock the lid in place and ensure that the valve is in sealing position.

3. Press the manual button to cook on high pressure for about 25 minutes.

4. When the time is up, use a natural pressure release for about 15 minutes.

5. Get turkey out from Instant Pot. Select sauté mode and set on high pressure. Boil the juices.

6. Using a small container, mix cornstarch and water until smooth; gradually pour into cooking juices. Cook and stir for 3 minutes.

7. When it is cool enough to handle, cut meat with two forks, return meat to Instant Pot and stir while you heat through.

8. Heat the Instant Pot. Open and split rolls, brush cut sides with butter.

9. Place on an ungreased baking sheet, cut side up. Bake until golden brown for about 10 minutes.

10. Pour $1/3$ cup of turkey mixture on roll bottoms.

11. Serve and enjoy!!!

Cuban Pulled Pork Sandwiches

Preparation time: 15 minutes

Cooking time: 30 minutes

Total time: 45 minutes

Servings: 15

Ingredients:

- 12 garlic cloves, minced
- 2 tsp. salt
- 2 tsp. pepper
- 1 tbsp. olive oil
- 1 cup of orange juice
- 2 tbsp. spiced rum, optional
- 2 tbsp. ground coriander
- 2 tsp. white pepper
- 1 tsp. cayenne pepper
- ½ cup of lime juice
- 1 boneless pork shoulder butt roast (5 lbs)

Sandwiches:

- 1 ½ lbs. Swiss cheese, sliced
- 2 loaves (1 lb each) French bread
- Yellow mustard, optional
- 16 dill pickle slices
- 1 ½ lbs. thinly sliced deli ham

Cooking instructions:

1. Divide pork into 2 pieces, season with salt and pepper.

2. Select sauté mode on your Instant Pot using high pressure.

3. Add oil; working in batches, fry pork to become brown on all sides and remove from cooker.

4. Add the orange and lime juices, stirring to scrape browned bits from bottom of Instant Pot.

5. Add the garlic, rum, if desired, coriander, white pepper and cayenne pepper. Return pork and any collected juices to cooker.

6. Close and lock the lid in place and ensure that the valve is in sealing position.

7. Press the manual function to cook on high pressure for about 20 minutes.

8. When the time is up, use a natural pressure release for about 8 minutes.

9. Carefully remove roast; when cool enough to handle, cut with two forks and get 1 cup cooking liquid from cooker, put to pork and toss.

10. Divide each loaf of bread in half lengthwise. You may spread mustard over cut sides of bread if you desire.

11. Layer bottom halves of bread with pickles, pork, ham and cheese.

12. Serve and enjoy!!!

Apple Bread with Salted Caramel Icing

Preparation time: 20 minutes

Cooking time: 1 hour 15 minutes

Total time: 1 hour 35 minutes

Calories: 545 kcal

Servings: 12

Ingredients:

- 4 cups of apples Peeled Cored, and cubed
- 1 cup of sugar
- 3 eggs
- 1 tbsp. vanilla
- 1 tbsp. apple pie spice
- 2 ½ cups of flour
- 1 stick butter
- 1 tbsp. baking powder

For the topping:

- 1 stick salted butter
- 2 cups of brown sugar
- 1 cup of heavy cream
- 2 cups of powdered sugar

Cooking Instructions:

1. Using your mixer, mix together eggs, butter, apple pie spice, and sugar until creamy and smooth.

2. Put your apples. Use another bowl and mix flour and baking powder. Add your flour mix to your wet mix.

3. If the batter was thick. Pour into your 7" spring form pan. Keep your trivet in the bottom of your Instant pot and one cup of water.

4. Close and lock the lid in place and ensure that the valve is in sealing position.

5. Press the manual button to cook on high pressure for about 72 minutes.

6. When the time is up, use a natural pressure release for about 25 minutes.

7. Carefully open the lid once the pressure has been released.

8. You can now remove and top with Icing.

9. Serve and enjoy!!!

Apple Crisp

Preparation time: 6 minutes

Cooking time: 8 minutes

Total time: 14 minutes

Servings: 5

Ingredients

- 2 ½ tsp. cinnamon
- ½ tsp. nutmeg
- ½ cup of water
- 1 tbsp. maple syrup
- 4 ½ tbsp. butter
- ¾ cup of old fashioned rolled oats
- ¼ cup of flour
- ¼ cup of brown sugar
- 5 medium sized apples, peeled and chopped into chunks
- ½ tsp. salt

Cooking Instructions:

1. Put apples on the bottom of your Instant Pot.

2. Pour in cinnamon and nutmeg. Top with water and maple syrup.

3. Heat the butter to melt. Using a small bowl, mix together melted butter, oats, flour, brown sugar and salt. You can drop by the spoonful on top of the apples.

4. Close and lock the lid in place and ensure that the valve is in sealing position.

5. Press the manual key to cook on high pressure for about 10 minutes.

6. When the time is up, use a natural pressure release for about 8 minutes.

7. Put your toppings like vanilla ice cream.

8. Serve and enjoy!!!

Mini-Lemon Cheesecakes
Preparation time: 8 minutes

Cooking time: 8 minutes

Total time: 16 minutes

Servings: 5

Ingredients:

- ½ tsp. vanilla
- 6 half pint mason jars
- 18 oz cream cheese, room temp
- ½ cup of sugar
- 1.5 cups of water
- 1 tsp. flour
- ¼ cup of sour cream, room temp
- 1 tbsp. Lemon Juice
- zest of one lemon
- 3 eggs, room temp
- 1 jar lemon curd (found in the jam & jelly aisle)
- Raspberries (optional)

Cooking Instructions:

1. In a large bowl, mix together cream cheese, sugar, and flour until mixture is creamy with no lumps.

2. Pour in vanilla, sour cream, lemon juice, and lemon zest just until mixed well. Beat in one egg at a time just until mixed. You may not need to overbeat.

3. Take each jar and filled with ¼ cup of cheesecake batter. Gently drop 1tbsp of lemon curd on top of batter.

4. Put an additional ¼ cup cheesecake batter to each jar on top of the lemon curd and cover each jar with foil in a loose way.

5. Put 1.5 cups of water to the bottom of the Instant Pot. Keep the trivet on the bottom.

6. Line up three jars on top of the trivet. Stack the other three jars on the first three.

7. Close and lock the lid in place and ensure that the valve is in sealing position.

8. Press the manual function to cook on high pressure for about 8 minutes.

9. When the time is up, use a natural pressure release for about 10 minutes.

10. Using a towel, carefully remove the jars from the Instant Pot, and allow it to cool and store in the refrigerator until ready to serve.

11. Garnish with additional lemon curd and raspberries.

12. Serve and enjoy!!!

Berries & Cream Breakfast Cake

Preparation time: 8 minutes

Cooking time: 10 minutes

Total time: 18 minutes

Servings: 5

Ingredients:

Breakfast Cake:

- 2 tsp. vanilla extract
- 6 eggs
- 1/3 cup of sugar
- Sweet Yogurt Glaze
- 2 tbsp. butter, melted
- 3/4 cup of ricotta cheese
- 3/4 cup of plain or vanilla yogurt
- 1/2 tsp. salt
- 2 tsp. baking powder
- 1/2 cup of Berry Compote
- Berry Compote (prepare and chill beforehand)
- 1 cup of whole wheat pastry flour or white whole wheat flour

Sweet Yogurt Glaze:

- 1/4 cup yogurt
- 1/2 tsp vanilla extract
- 1 tsp milk
- 2 tbsp powdered sugar

Cooking Instructions:

1. Make the Berry Compote beforehand first so it is cold and thick because if used warm, it has a tendency to sink to the bottom of the pan.

2. For the Breakfast Cake, generously grease a 6 cup Bundt pan with nonstick cooking spray.

3. Mix together the eggs and sugar until smooth. Put the butter, ricotta cheese, yogurt, and vanilla and mix until smooth.

4. Using a different container, whisk together the flour, salt, and baking powder. Combine with the egg mixture. Pour into the prepared Bundt pan.

5. With a half cup of Berry Compote, drop by tbsp on top of the batter and swirl in with a knife.

6. Put a cup of water to the Instant Pot and place a trivet inside. Keep the Bundt pan on the trivet.

7. Close and lock the lid in place and ensure that the valve is in sealing position. Press the manual button to cook on high pressure for about 30 minutes.

8. Prepare the Sweet Yogurt Glaze while the cake is cooking by whisking together the yogurt, vanilla, milk, and powdered sugar; keep aside.

9. When the time is up, use a natural pressure release for about 10 minutes.

10. Carefully remove pan from Instant Pot. Allow it to cool. Loosen the sides of the cake from the pan and gently turn over onto a plate.

11. Serve warm and enjoy.

Apple & Ricotta Cake

Preparation time: 8 minutes

Cooking time: 22 minutes

Total time: 30 minutes

Servings: 7

Ingredients:

- 2 cups of water
- 2 apples, 1 sliced 1 diced
- 1 tbsp. lemon juice
- ¼ cup of raw sugar
- 2 eggs
- 1 cup of ricotta cheese
- ⅓ cup of sugar
- 3 tbsp. extra-virgin olive oil
- 1 tsp. vanilla extract
- 1 cup of all-purpose flour
- ⅛ tsp. cinnamon
- 2 tsp. baking powder
- 1 tsp. baking soda

Cooking Instructions:

1. Put water to the base of pressure cooker, plus steamer basket and keep aside.

2. Slice one apple and mince the other and cover with lemon juice.

3. Make a shallow and wide 4-cup capacity heat-proof bowl by adding a disk of wax paper at the bottom, oiling and dusting all the inside with flour.

4. Spray the base of the bowl with raw sugar and arrange the sliced apples in the bowl.

5. In a small bowl, mix together egg, ricotta, sugar, olive oil and vanilla using a fork. Then, spray the flour, cinnamon, baking powder and baking soda in the mixing container using a flour sifter.

6. Using a regular blender, blend well with a fork and then put the apple dices. Pour into prepared bowl and lower into the pressure cooker without covering.

7. Close and lock the lid in place and ensure that the valve is in sealing position. Press the manual button to cook on high pressure for about 25 minutes.

8. When the time is up, use a natural pressure release for about 15 minutes. Carefully open the lid once the pressure has been released.

9. Taste if the cake is done by inserting a toothpick in the middle - if it comes out dirty lower back into the pressure and cook for a few more minutes.

10. Remove the cake and place in a serving plate.

11. Serve and enjoy!!!

Applesauce

Preparation time: 3 minutes

Cooking time: 9 minutes

Total time: 12 minutes

Calories: 140 kcal

Servings: 5

Ingredients:

- 1 cup of water
- 2 drops cinnamon essential oil
- 1 tsp. organic cinnamon optional
- 7 medium to large apples Granny Smith, Gala, McIntosh, Fuji, etc.

Cooking Instructions:

1. Slice apples into 2-inch chunks. Throw away the core, stem and seeds.

2. Put them in Instant Pot along with 1 cup of water.

3. Close and lock the lid in place and ensure that the valve is in sealing position.

4. Press the manual button to cook on high pressure for about 9 minutes.

5. When the time is up, use a natural pressure release for about 3 minutes.

6. Turn steam vent to release pressure. Carefully open the lid when all steam has evaporated.

7. Using immersion blender, blend to smooth out applesauce to your taste.

8. Put 2 drops of cinnamon oil or powder to taste.

9. Allow it to cool or put in the refrigerator.

10. Serve and enjoy!!!

Homemade Pumpkin Puree

Preparation time: 5 minutes

Cooking time: 14 minutes

Total time: 19 minutes

Servings: 5

Ingredients:

- 4 lbs. pie pumpkin
- 1 cup of water

Cooking Instructions

1. Remove the stem from the pumpkin.

2. Put a steamer basket in the bottom of the Instant Pot and put 1 cup of water.

3. Put the pumpkin on the basket cover the lid without touching the top of the pumpkin.

4. Close and lock the lid in place and ensure that the valve is in sealing position. Press the manual key to cook on high pressure for about 15 minutes.

5. When the time is up, use a natural pressure release for about 8 minutes. Carefully open the lid once the pressure has been released.

6. Remove the pumpkin from the Instant Pot (use the handles of the rack) and place on a cutting board. Allow it to cool until it is easy to handle.

7. Cut the pumpkin into half, remove the seeds, goop, and peel off the skin.

8. Using a regular blender, blend the soft pumpkin until smooth and add a tablespoon of water, if needed to help it along.

9. Serve and enjoy!

ACKNOWLEDGEMENT

In preparing the **"The Instant Pot Recipes Cookbook"**, I sincerely wish to acknowledge my indebtedness to my husband Mr. Michael Foreman for his support and the wholehearted cooperation and vast experience of my two colleagues - Mrs. Nicole Walker and Mrs. Barbara Jones.

SHELLEY FOREMAN

Made in the USA
Middletown, DE
02 November 2018